T0150376

RACE & ECONOMICS

RACE & ECONOMICS

How much can be blamed on discrimination?

Walter E. Williams

HOOVER INSTITUTION PRESS

Stanford University ▪ *Stanford, California*

With its eminent scholars and world-renowned library and archives, the
Hoover Institution seeks to improve the human condition by advancing
ideas that promote economic opportunity and prosperity, while securing and
safeguarding peace for America and all mankind. The views expressed in its
publications are entirely those of the authors and do not necessarily reflect the
views of the staff, officers, or Board of Overseers of the Hoover Institution.

hoover.org

Hoover Institution Press Publication No. 599

Hoover Institution at Leland Stanford Junior University,
Stanford, California 94305-6003

First printing 2011
26 25 24 23 22 21   10 9 8 7 6 5

Cataloging-in-Publication Data is available from the Library of Congress.
ISBN 978-0-8179-1244-4 (cloth)
ISBN 978-0-8179-1245-1 (pbk)
ISBN 978-0-8179-1246-8 (epub)
ISBN 978-0-8179-1247-5 (mobi)
ISBN 978-0-8179-1248-2 (ePDF)

To the memory of all those Americans,
both black and white but now long dead,
who shed their blood, sweat, and tears to
help our nation live up to the letter and spirit
of the principles of its founding documents.

Contents

Acknowledgments

This work is a result of a number of years gathering research materials, writing, and letting the manuscript sit; gathering more materials, writing, and letting the manuscript sit before I finally accepted an invitation for it to be published. The manuscript has benefited immensely from my exchange of ideas with my longtime friend and associate Thomas Sowell of the Hoover Institution. I want to thank the librarians at Villanova University and George Mason University Law School for their assistance. I am also indebted to the patience and encouragement of Connie Williams, my now-deceased wife. Finally, a word of thanks to Kathleen Spolarich, my assistant, who typed up numerous drafts of the manuscript.

Walter E. Williams
John M. Olin Distinguished
Professor of Economics,
George Mason University

Preface

RACIAL ISSUES OFTEN GIVE RISE to high emotions but little understanding. The black experience in America naturally creates a temptation to think of today's black experience in terms of white racism and oppression. My purpose in writing this book is to apply simple economic analysis to some of the problems that black Americans have faced in the past and still face today. There is no question that they suffered gross violations of basic human rights in the forms of chattel slavery, discrimination under Jim Crow laws and customs, and personal violence—lynching, beatings, and arson. But an acknowledgment of and consensus on those injustices, and on residual discrimination, do not carry us very far in evaluating what is or is not in the best interest of blacks nowadays.

One of the things that economics brings to the analysis is explicit recognition that people will not engage in activities—including racial discrimination—no matter what the cost. Although racial discrimination imposes costs on those discriminated against, the person or entity doing the discriminating also bears costs. Recognizing that, along with the generalization that people instinctively seek to *reduce* costs, suggests that one of the contributions economics can make is to analyze methods a discriminator uses to reduce them.

I shall argue that free-market resource allocation, as opposed to allocation on political grounds, is in the interests of minorities and/or less-preferred individuals. This assertion is not simply a matter of ideological preference; there is evidence for it. In markets, because their transactions are mostly an individual affair, it is unnecessary to win the approval or permission of others; the costs and benefits are a private matter. In free markets, people can register the intensity of their preference. For example, if a person wants a particular job, he can indicate how much he wants it by bidding down the wage he is willing to accept. If renting an apartment, he can offer a higher price. The market encompasses a sort of parity non-existent in the political arena, where one person's dollar has the same power as anyone else's.

Contrast these features of market-resource allocation with those of the political arena. In the latter, minorities cannot realize a particular preference unless they win over the majority. In addition, each citizen has only one vote, which means that, unlike in the free market, he cannot register the intensity of his preference. Further, increased concentration of political power at the national level handicaps minorities in the sense that their votes become more diluted. For example, blacks comprise about 44 percent of the population of Philadelphia but 13 percent of the population of the United States. The concentration of black votes—bloc voting—is therefore far more influential in Philadelphia's political decision-making arena than in the national one. The greater the number of decisions that are made nationally, the smaller the significance of black votes will be. As a generality, if one is a member of a minority, he is less likely to realize his preferences if decisions are made in the political arena, particularly if they are made at the national level.

Consider another comparison between market- and political-resource allocation. If one tours a low-income black neighborhood, he will see people wearing some nice clothing, eating some nice food, driving some nice cars, and he might even see some nice houses—but no nice schools. Why? The answer relates directly to how clothing, food, cars, and houses—versus schools—are allocated. Clothing, food, cars, and houses are allocated through the market mechanism. Schools, for the most part, are parceled out through the political mechanism. If a buyer is dissatisfied with goods distributed in the market, the individual can simply "fire" the producer by taking his business elsewhere. If a buyer (taxpayer) is dissatisfied with a public school, such an option is not, in a black neighborhood, economically available to him. He has to bear the burden of moving to a neighborhood with better schools. Interestingly, if one does see high-quality schools in poor or moderate-income black neighborhoods, they tend to be private institutions, such as Ivy Leaf in Philadelphia, Marcus Garvey in Los Angeles, and Marva Collins Prep in Chicago.

Some might argue that it is unfair for people (as in the case of wages) to have to charge a cheaper price for what they sell or pay a higher price (as in the case of rent) for what they buy. Economic theory as such cannot answer questions of fairness. However, economic theory can predict the effects of not permitting some people to charge lower prices for what they sell and pay higher prices for what they buy. As we shall see by the evidence marshaled in this book, they will be worse off than otherwise would be the case.

Unlike in prior times, most blacks are not poor, but a large percentage still are. Decent people promote policy in the name of helping the poor and disadvantaged. Those policies can make their ostensible beneficiaries worse off, because policy is often evaluated in terms of intentions rather than effects. That is a direct result of how people view the world. Consider popular support for increases in the minimum wage. If one believes that an employer must hire a certain number of workers to get a particular job done, an increase in minimum wage means that workers will earn higher wages and employers lower profits. However, if the visionary sees employers finding *substitutes* for higher-priced workers—such as automation or relocating to a lower-wage environment—he might oppose increases in the minimum wage on the grounds it will cause unemployment for some workers. Compassionate policy requires dispassionate analysis. Policy intentions and policy effects often bear no relationship to one another.

After finishing this book, a reader might be compelled to ask what can be done to help. My answer would be similar to that given by abolitionist Frederick Douglass, during a Boston speech at a meeting of the Massachusetts Anti-Slavery Society in April 1865. The speech bore the title, "What the Black Man Wants," and in it, Douglass said:

> Everybody has asked the question, and they learned to ask it early of the abolitionists, 'What shall we do with the Negro?' I have had but one answer from the beginning. Do nothing with us! Your doing with us has already played the mischief with us. Do nothing with us! If the apples will not remain on the tree of their own strength, if they are worm-eaten

at the core, if they are early ripe and disposed to fall, let them fall! I am not for tying or fastening them on the tree in any way, except by nature's plan, and if they will not stay there, let them fall.

And if the Negro cannot stand on his own legs, let him fall also. All I ask is, give him a chance to stand on his own legs! Let him alone! If you see him on his way to school, let him alone, don't disturb him! If you see him going to the dinner table at a hotel, let him go! If you see him going to the ballot box, let him alone, don't disturb him! If you see him going into a workshop, just let him alone—your interference is doing him a positive injury.

■　■　■

CHAPTER 1

Blacks Today and Yesterday

BLACK AMERICANS, COMPARED WITH any other racial group, have come the greatest distance, over some of the highest hurdles, in a shorter period of time. This unprecedented progress can be verified through several measures. If one were to total black earnings and consider black Americans a separate nation, he would find that, in 2008, they earned $726 billion. That would make them the world's sixteenth-richest nation, just behind Turkey but ahead of Poland, Belgium, and Switzerland. (See Table 1.1 on the next page.)

Individual feats, in terms of "power," are equally impressive. Black Americans are, and have been, chief executives of some of the world's largest and richest cities, such as New York, Chicago, Los Angeles, Philadelphia, and Washington, D.C. It was a black American, General Colin Powell, appointed head of the Joint Chiefs of Staff in October 1989, who directed the world's mightiest military and later became U.S. secretary of state. And he was succeeded by Condoleezza Rice, of the same race and national origin. As a group, black Americans include many of the world's richest and most famous personalities.

On the eve of the Civil War, it is doubtful whether a slave or a slave owner would have believed these gains possible in less than a century and a half, if ever. That progress speaks well not only for the sacrifices and intestinal fortitude of a people but also of a nation in which the gains were possible. One cannot imagine any other nation in which these gains could have been achieved. However, if one listens to spokesmen for civil rights organizations, self-anointed black leaders, and various politicians, one would get a different impression about black progress.

Table 1.1. Country Gross Domestic Product, 2008, by rank

Country	Rank	GDP*	Country	Rank	GDP*
USA	1	14,093,310	Mexico	13	1,088,128
Japan	2	4,910,840	Australia	14	1,015,217
China	3	4,326,996	Korea, Rep.	15	929,121
Germany	4	3,649,494	Netherlands	16	871,004
France	5	2,856,556	Turkey	17	734,853
United Kingdom	6	2,674,057	**Black Americans**	**18**	**726,059**
Italy	7	2,303,079	Poland	19	527,866
Russian Federation	8	1,679,484	Indonesia	20	510,730
Spain	9	1,604,235	Belgium	21	504,206
Brazil	10	1,575,151	Switzerland	22	491,950
Canada	11	1,501,329	Sweden	23	478,961
India	12	1,159,171			

* in millions of U.S. dollars

Note: As a proxy for black GDP, per capita income ($18,054) in 2008 was multiplied by the number (40,216,000) of blacks who lived in the U.S. in the same year.

Data Sources: World Bank, *Population and Per Capita Money Income, Black: 1967 to 2008.* siteresources.worldbank.org/DATASTATISTICS/Resources/GDP.pdf (accessed May 20, 2010); www.census.gov/hhes/www/income/histinc/incpertoc.html.

It is indeed true that for many black Americans, such gains have proved elusive. The U.S. Census Bureau classifies those people, who represent perhaps 30 percent of the black population, as poor. Poverty among them today differs significantly from their poverty of yesteryear. There is a difference between material poverty and what may be called behavioral or spiritual poverty. The former is a money measure that the census bureau in 2006 defined as $20,444 for an urban family of four.[1] The latter, on the other hand, refers to conduct and values that prevent the development of healthy families, a work ethic, and self-sufficiency. The absence of those values virtually guarantees pathological lifestyles that include drug and alcohol addiction, crime, violence, incarceration, illegitimacy, single-parent households, dependency, and erosion of the work ethic.

For the most part, material poverty is no longer the problem it once was. Generally, people whom the census bureau defines as poor have almost the same level of consumption of protein, vitamins and other nutrients as upper middle-income people.[2] In 1971, only about 32 percent of all Americans enjoyed air conditioning in their homes; by 2001, 76 percent of *poor* people enjoyed that comforting amenity. In 1971, 43 percent of all

American households owned a color television set. By 2001, 97 percent of poor households had a color television set and over half of those, two or more sets. Forty-six percent of poor households now own their homes, and only about 6 percent of them are overcrowded. Indeed, the average poor American has more living space than the average *non*poor individual living in Paris, London, Vienna, Athens, and other European cities.[3]

Money measures of poverty seriously understate income, because they omit in-kind transfers, such as food stamps and medical and housing assistance. And even money measures are suspect. As early as 1990, it was estimated that the poor were spending an average of $1.94 for every dollar in welfare income received.[4] That additional income might have come from unreported employment, or illegal activities.

While material poverty in its historical or global form is nonexistent in the U.S., what I call behavioral poverty has skyrocketed. Female-headed households increased from 18 percent of the black population in 1950 to well over 68 percent by 2000.[5] As of 2002, 53 percent of black children lived in single-parent households, compared to 20 percent for whites.[6] As of 2006, roughly 45 percent of blacks fifteen or older had never been married, in addition to 17 percent who had been divorced or widowed; that contrasts with only 27 percent of whites fifteen and older never married and 16 percent divorced or widowed.[7]

Some argue that today's weak black-family structure is a "legacy" of slavery. Such an explanation loses credibility when one examines evidence from the past. Even during slavery, where marriage was forbidden, most black children lived in biological two-parent families. One study of nineteenth-century slave families found that in as many as three-fourths of them, all the children had the same mother and father.[8] In New York City, in 1925, 85 percent of kin-related black households were two-parent households.[9] In fact, "Five in six children under the age of six lived with both parents."[10]

A study of 1880 family structure in Philadelphia shows that three-quarters of all black families were nuclear (composed of two parents and children). What is significant, given today's arguments that slavery and discrimination decimated the black family, is the fact that years ago there were only slight differences in family structure between racial groups. The percentages of nuclear families were: black (75.2 percent), Irish (82.2), German (84.5), and native white American (73.1).[11] Only one-quarter of black families were headed by females. Female-headed families among Irish, German, and native white Americans averaged 11 percent.

Also significant was the fact that, in 1847, just one of ten Philadelphia blacks had been born in slavery. However, those ex-slave families were *more* likely than free-born blacks to be two-parent families.[12] Theodore Hershberg found that 90 percent of households in which the head purchased his freedom included two parents. He found that those households existed 80 percent of the time among ex-slaves in general and 77 percent of the time among free-born blacks.[13] Historian Herbert Gutman found, in analyzing data on families in Harlem between 1905 and 1925, that only 3 percent of all families "were headed by a woman under thirty."[14]

Thomas Sowell reported that, "Going back a hundred years, when blacks were just one generation out of slavery, we find that census data of that era showed that a slightly higher percentage of black adults had married than white adults. This fact remained true in every census from 1890 to 1940."[15]

Coupled with the dramatic breakdown in the black-family structure has been an astonishing growth in the rate of illegitimacy. The black rate was only 19 percent in 1940, but skyrocketed in the late 1960s, reaching 49 percent in 1975.[16] As of 2000, black illegitimacy stood at 68 percent and in some cities over 80 percent.[17] High illegitimacy rates not only spell poverty and dependency but also contribute to the social pathology seen in many black communities: high incidences of adolescent violence and predatory sex, and as sociologist Charles Murray has noted, a community not unlike that portrayed in *Lord of the Flies*.[18]

Several studies point to welfare programs as a major contributor to several aspects of behavioral poverty. One of these early studies was the Seattle/Denver Income Maintenance Experiment, also known as the "SIME/DIME" study. Among its findings: for each dollar increase in welfare payment, low-income persons reduced labor earning by eighty cents.[19] Using 1979 National Longitudinal Survey of Youth data, Ann Hill and June O'Neill found that a 50 percent increase in the monthly value of welfare benefits led to a 43 percent increase in the number of out-of-wedlock births.[20]

We can see some of the effects of welfare on the work experience of poor families. In 1959, 31.5 percent of heads of poor families worked full-time year-round; by 1989, the percentage had fallen to 16.2. In 1959,

30.5 percent did not work at all (either full-time or part-time); by 1989, that figure had risen to 50.8 percent. Some argue that such high unemployment stems from lack of job opportunities in inner cities. That observation is questionable. During 1979–1980, the National Bureau of Economic Research conducted a survey in the ghettos of Boston, Philadelphia, and Chicago. Only a minority of the respondents were employed, yet almost as many said it was easy or fairly easy to get a job as a laborer as said it was difficult or impossible; and 71 percent said it was fairly easy to get a minimum-wage job.[21]

Despite frequent assertions to the contrary, many of the seemingly intractable problems encountered by a significant number of black Americans do not result from racial discrimination. This is not to say discrimination does not exist. Nor is it to say discrimination has no adverse effects. For policy purposes, however, the issue is not whether or not racial discrimination exists but the extent to which it explains what we see today. For example, it is clear that low academic achievement by black youngsters poses serious handicaps. If we assume that the problem is one of racial discrimination, where blacks are being denied educational opportunities, then civil rights strategies might produce a solution. However, if poor educational achievement is a result of other factors, resources spent pursuing a civil rights strategy will yield disappointing results.

The thrust of the argument in the chapters that follow is that the most difficult problems black Americans face, particularly those who are poor, cannot adequately be explained by current racial discrimination. Instead, most problems are self-inflicted or, as will be the major focus of this book, a result of policies, regulations, and restrictions emanating from federal, state, and local governments. I will argue that free markets and the profit motive have not reduced opportunities. The drivers have instead been the power of vested interest groups to use, as a means to greater wealth, the coercive powers of government to stifle market competition.

Free markets and the profit motive, far from being enemies to blacks, have been friends. The reason is quite simple. Customers prefer lower prices to higher prices, and businessmen prefer higher profits to lower profits. The most effective tools for a seller to gain a customer are to offer a lower price and better services than his competitor. Similarly, the most effective tool for a worker to get an employer to hire him is to offer to accept a lower wage (with wages being a form of pricing). Many employers will find higher profits a more attractive alternative to indulging personal preferences or maintaining racial loyalty.

The ability to prevent a less-preferred worker from accepting a lower wage is one of the most effective tools in the arsenal of racists everywhere. Racial antipathy is not a necessary, nor even the primary, incentive for using government power to prevent others from offering a lower price. People simply want to earn higher income and profits. The use of government restrictions, violence, or intimidation to prevent others from competing and offering prices below the "desired" price is consistent with that end. The fact that some blacks were able to earn a comfortable living and indeed become prosperous — in both the antebellum South, in the face of slavery and grossly discriminatory laws, and the North, where there was at best only weak enforcement of civil rights — gives strong testament to the power of the market as a friend to blacks.

Further evidence of the free market as a friend is suggested by all the legislation and extra-legal measures taken to prevent free, peaceable, voluntary exchange between blacks and whites. After all, why would laws and extra-legal measures be necessary to restrict whites from hiring blacks or blacks from selling to whites, or whites serving blacks in restaurants, if whites did not want to make these transactions in the first place? Whenever one sees laws written, or extra-legal measures taken, to prevent an activity, he should immediately suspect that not everyone would voluntarily behave according to those legal requirements.

In short, market restrictions are a far more important limitation on black socioeconomic progress than racial discrimination, a theme that will be developed in succeeding chapters.

CHAPTER 2

Is Discrimination a Complete Barrier to Economic Mobility?

TO OBSERVE RACIAL DISCRIMINATION is one thing. Quite another is to ask whether it is an insurmountable barrier to socioeconomic advancement. If a given level of discrimination is not insurmountable, then spending resources to eliminate every vestige of it would be wasted, because those resources might be more productively used elsewhere to promote the same kind of advancement.

Racial as well as religious conflict has existed in varying degrees since the founding of the United States, and throughout the world for centuries. In addition to black Americans, the Irish, Italians, Jews, Puerto Ricans, Poles, Chinese, Japanese, Swedish, and most other ethnic groups have shared the experience of being discriminated against by one means or another.[1] The extent of discrimination they have faced has differed in degree and kind. Similarly, the response of these groups *to* discrimination has varied between and even within them.

As highly publicized as racial conflict is in the United States, what seems to be less appreciated is that such conflict is a phenomenon unique neither to this country nor to the twentieth century. Racial and ethnic preference, grouping, and conflict have been a permanent global feature of man's history.

In England, there has been widespread discrimination against West Indians, Pakistanis, and Indians.[2] South Africa has a history of societal bifurcation and mutual hostility between Britons, Afrikaners, Asians, Coloreds, and black Africans, much of which continues today despite the end of apartheid.

Contrary to what is often thought, no racial or ethnic group has a monopoly on racial oppression and discrimination. Colored peoples racially discriminate against whites as well as other colored peoples. In Africa, black Africans often do so against Arabs, Syrians, Lebanese, Indians, and Chinese.[3] Recent history has seen the expulsion en masse of some 50,000 Asians from Uganda.[4] There have also been mass expulsions of Asians from Kenya.[5] Although not nearly as extreme as in those two nations, Asians have encountered racial discrimination and hostility in the other countries of East Africa and Southern Africa, such as Tanzania, Zambia, and Malawi.[6]

In addition, there is discrimination and conflict between people of identical racial stock but of different ethnic and religious groups. Widely known examples, which have resulted in large-scale murder, include Irish Catholics versus Irish Protestants; Igbos versus Hausa in Nigeria;[7] Tutsis versus Hutus in Burundi; and Kikuyus and Luos in Kenya. The Tutsi massacre in 1972 saw an estimated 80,000 to 150,000 Hutus slaughtered; the atrocities included dismemberment and decapitation.[8] According to a United Nations report, about 800,000 people were killed in the Rwandan genocide in 1994.[9]

Other examples of ethnic conflict, some of it violent, can be found in Lebanon, with the Muslims versus Christians; Belgium, with the Flemings versus the Walloons; Sri Lanka, with the Singhalese versus the Tamils; Israel, with Palestinians versus Jews; and Canada, with English-speaking versus French-speaking populations.

Chinese in Southeast Asia

In some countries of Southeast Asia, the minority Chinese population suffers the status of most-despised minority.[10] In that region, the Chinese have always constituted a small presence—no more than 10 percent of the entire Southeast Asian population—and numbering less than 3 percent in countries such as Indonesia and the Philippines. The hostility of the indigenous populations has historically been manifested by massacre or deportation of segments of the Chinese population.[11]

No less remarkable than the hostile racial climate the Chinese face in Southeast Asia is their considerable economic strength; through their roles as middlemen, merchants, and money handlers, they produce 30 to

40 percent of Indonesia's national product—at least ten times as much as their share of the population.[12] A similarly disproportionate economic predominance can be seen in most other countries of Southeast Asia—for example, the Philippines, Malaysia,[13] and Thailand.[14] In Malaysia, where the Chinese constitute a much larger proportion of the population (37 percent), they own four-fifths of all retail establishments and three-fifths of all non-foreign-owned, corporate-equity capital invested in the country.[15]

Numerous measures have been undertaken to reduce the economic predominance of the Chinese in Southeast Asia. These measures have ranged from affirmative action and outright expropriation of property to job-reservation laws and harsh business-licensing requirements.[16] Despite measures to restrict the enterprise of the Chinese, their population clearly enjoyed a higher standard of living.[17] Malays, for example, have never earned more than 57 percent of Chinese median income.[18]

Despite anti-Chinese discriminatory laws, there is wholesale evasion of the anti-Chinese discriminatory laws. In many enterprises reserved for the indigenous population, what appears to be indigenous ownership and control is really a front or a stand-in for a Chinese owner. Such enterprises are often referred to as "Ali Baba" companies, with Ali being the apparent indigenous owner and Baba being the Chinese real owner. These scams survive with the connivance and participation of corrupt officials charged with the enforcement of the discriminatory laws.

Racial Malevolence and Economic Progress

No attempt is being made here to completely examine racial/ethnic hostility. I only want to (1) establish its widespread existence and (2) show that, despite handicaps wrought by discrimination, economic progress is possible. Obvious examples are the Chinese, Indians, and Jews—all despised aliens in racially hostile climates. A fuller examination would suggest that the same is true of Armenians, Greeks, and Jews in the successor states of the Ottoman Empire, and Igbos in Nigeria. The fact that such alien minorities sometimes make significant economic gains questions at least two assumptions made in the literature on race. Benevolence on behalf of the larger society is neither a necessary nor sufficient condition for an ethnic minority to achieve economic predominance;[19] and economic progress can occur in the absence of what is traditionally considered political power.[20]

Obviously, if the dominant racial group expropriates all the wealth of the non-preferred group, such as under a system of slavery, the latter has little or no chance to make economic progress. But in less extreme cases, the effect of racial hostility on group progress is not so clear.

The elimination of racial discrimination has been one prescription for economic progress and political power another. The experiences of the Chinese in Southeast Asia, Indians in Africa, and Armenians in the post-Ottoman Empire show that neither the elimination of racial discrimination nor political power is a *necessary* condition for group economic progress. In our own country, we have seen how Jews have prospered in the face of hostility. Although they now have significant political clout, their strongest socioeconomic progress occurred at a time when they were politically unimportant, even in areas where they were most highly concentrated.[21]

Japanese-Americans and Chinese-Americans have always been and continue to be politically insignificant. On the West Coast, they were subjected to harsh persecution. The Chinese Exclusion Act of 1882, which proscribed citizenship,[22] set the Japanese up for denial of land ownership. California, in 1913, enacted an anti-Japanese land law.[23] Under its terms, a person ineligible for citizenship could not own agricultural land or lease it for more than three years. Over the ensuing years, ten other Western states adopted California's policy. The U.S. Supreme Court upheld the constitutionality of these state laws.[24] During World War II, Japanese were interned, and their property was virtually confiscated.

Without a doubt, Japanese (and Chinese) have had experiences in the United States that, at least according to conventional wisdom, make them prime candidates for status as a disadvantaged group. Yet by almost any measure, they are one of the most "successful" ethnic groups in America. As early as 1975, Japanese-Americans had the following characteristics: 19.5 percent of those employed were professional workers compared to 15.6 percent of white workers (the Chinese had 25 percent); their unemployment rate was 2.4 percent versus 4.1 percent for whites; similarly, in terms of labor-force participation rates and years of education, the Japanese and Chinese surpassed that of the white population.[25] By contrast, although the Irish rank among the most politically successful of U.S.

ethnic groups, by every measure of socioeconomic status they compare unfavorably to the Japanese, Jews, and Chinese.

The experience of several ethnic minority groups in the United States and elsewhere seriously calls into question arguments that disadvantaged minorities in the United States *must* acquire political power and need measures to "end racism" in order for socioeconomic growth to occur. The importance of recognizing that political power and/or social benevolence is not a necessary condition for the socioeconomic progress of an ethnic group is not only an important intellectual exercise but also has practical importance, because all activities require resource expenditure. If, for example, resources are spent for political organization, they cannot be spent, perhaps more productively, elsewhere.

Early Black Economic Achievement

The portrayal of blacks as helpless victims of slavery and later gross discrimination has become part of the popular wisdom. But the facts of the matter do not square with that portrayal.

Despite the brutal and oppressive nature of slavery, slaves did not quietly acquiesce. Many found ways to lessen slavery's hardships and attain a measure of independence. During colonial days, slaves learned skills and found that they could earn a measure of independence by servicing ships as rope makers, coopers, and shipwrights. Some entered more skilled trades, such as silversmithing, gold beating, and cabinetmaking.

Typically, slaves turned over a portion of their earnings to their owners in exchange for de facto freedom. This practice, called self-hire, generated criticism. "As early as 1733–34, a Charles Town, South Carolina, grand jury criticized slaveholders for allowing their slaves 'to work out by the Week,' and 'bring in a certain Hire' which was not only Contrary to a Law subsisting, but a Great Inlet to Idleness, Drunkenness and other Enormities."[26] Later, a group of Virginia planters said, "Many persons have suffered their slaves to go about to hire themselves and pay their masters for their hire,' and as a result 'certain' slaves lived free from their master's control."[27] "Two ambitious Charles Town bricklayers, Tony and Primus, who spent their days building a church under the supervision of their master, secretly rented themselves to local builders at night and on weekends."[28]

Many slaves exhibited great entrepreneurial spirit despite their handicaps. Even slave women were often found growing and selling produce in the South Carolina and Georgia Low Country. After putting in a day's work, some slaves were allowed to raise their own crops and livestock. These efforts allowed them to gain a presence in much of the marketing network on the streets and docks of port cities.[29] Ultimately, the South Carolina General Assembly passed a law requiring that slave-grown crops and livestock be sold only to the master. However, the law was very difficult to enforce, particularly among blacks who had gained knowledge of the marketplace. Market activity by slaves was so great that North Carolina whites mounted a campaign to stop slave "dealing and Trafficking" altogether. In 1741, that state passed a law prohibiting slaves from buying, selling, trading, or bartering "any Commodities whatsoever" or to raise hogs, cattle, or horses "on any Pretense whatsoever."[30]

During the colonial period, some slaves bought their freedom and acquired property. In Virginia's Northampton County, 44 out of 100 blacks had gained their freedom by 1664, and some had become landowners.[31] During the late eighteenth century, blacks could boast of owning land. James Pendarvis owned 3,250 acres in St. Paul's Parish in the Charleston District of South Carolina. Pendarvis also possessed 113 slaves. Cabinetmaker John Gough owned several buildings in Charleston and others in the coastal South.[32] During the late eighteenth and early nineteenth centuries, free blacks in Charleston had established themselves as relatively independent from an economic standpoint. As early as 1819, they comprised thirty types of workers, including ten tailors, eleven carpenters, twenty-two seamstresses, six shoemakers, and one hotel owner. Thirty years later, there were fifty types, including fifty carpenters, forty-three tailors, nine shoemakers, and twenty-one butchers.[33]

New Orleans had the largest population of free blacks in the Deep South. Though they could not vote, they enjoyed more rights than blacks in other parts of the South—such as the right to travel freely and to testify in court against white people. "They owned some $2 million worth of property and dominated skilled crafts like bricklaying, cigar making, carpentry, and shoe making."[34] New Orleans blacks also created privately supported benevolent societies, schools, and orphanages to assist their impoverished brethren.

Black entrepreneurs in New Orleans owned small businesses like liquor, grocery, and general stores capitalized with a few hundred dollars. There were also some larger businesses, for example, grocers like Francis Snaer, A. Blandin, and G. N. Ducroix, each of whom was worth over $10,000 ($209,000 in today's currency). One of the best-known black businesses was owned by Cecee Macarty, who inherited $12,000 and parlayed it into a business worth $155,000 at the time of her death in 1845. Another was Thorny Lafon, who started out with a small dry-goods store and later became a real estate dealer, amassing a fortune valued over $400,000 ($8 million today) by the time he died.[35] Black control of the cigar industry enabled men like Lucien Mansion and Georges Alces to own sizable factories, with Alces hiring as many as 200 men. Twenty-two black men listed themselves as factory owners in the New Orleans registry of free Negroes, though it is likely that most of these were one-man shops.[36]

Pierre A. D. Casenave, an immigrant from Santo Domingo, was among New Orleans' more notable businessmen. Having inherited $10,000, as a result of being a confidential clerk of a white merchant-philanthropist, Casenave was in the "commission" business by 1853. By 1857, he was worth $30,000 to $40,000, and he had built an undertaking business, catering mostly to whites, that was worth $2 million in today's dollars.[37]

Most free blacks in New Orleans were unskilled laborers. Males were employed on steamboats and as dockworkers and domestic servants, while females found work largely as domestic servants or washwomen. However, the ratio of skilled to unskilled workers among blacks was greater than among Irish and German workers. Indeed, free blacks dominated certain skilled crafts. According to J. D. B. DeBow, director of the 1850 census, in New Orleans that year there were 355 carpenters, 325 masons, 156 cigar makers, ninety-two shoemakers, sixty-one clerks, fifty-two mechanics, forty-three coopers, forty-one barbers, thirty-nine carmen, and twenty-eight painters.

In addition, there were free Negro blacksmiths (fifteen), butchers (eighteen), cabinetmakers (nineteen), cooks (twenty-five), overseers (eleven), ship carpenters (six), stewards (nine), and upholsterers (eight).[38] Robert C. Reinders, a historian, says that DeBow may have exaggerated the data to show that New Orleans had more skilled blacks than elsewhere; however, other evidence points to free-black prominence in skilled trades—for example, 540 skilled blacks signing a register to stay in the state between 1842 and 1861. Plus, travelers spoke of "Negro artisans being served by Irish waiters and free Negro masons with Irish hod carriers."[39] A few black skilled workers were relatively prosperous. Peter Howard, a porter, and C. Cruisin, an engraver, were each worth between $10,000 and $20,000. A. Tescault, a bricklayer, owned personal and real property valued at nearly $40,000.[40]

By the end of the antebellum era, there was considerable property ownership among slaves in both the Upper and Lower South. Many amassed their resources through the "task" (or "hiring-out") system. In Richmond and Petersburg, Virginia, slaves worked in tobacco factories and earned $150 to $200 a year, plus all expenses. By 1850, slave hiring was common in hemp manufacturing and in the textile and tobacco industries. In Richmond, 62 percent of the male slave force was hired; in Lynchburg, 52 percent, in Norfolk, more than 50 percent, and in Louisville, 24 percent. Across the entire South, at least 100,000 slaves were hired out each year.

Self-hiring was another practice with a long tradition. It benefited both the slave and slave owner. The latter did not have to pay for the slave's lodging and clothing. Slaves, although obligated to pay their masters a monthly or yearly fee, could keep for themselves what they earned above that amount. Frederick Douglass explained that while employed as a Baltimore ship's caulker, "I was to be allowed all my time; to make bargains for work; to find my own employment, and collect my own wages; and in return for this liberty, I was to pay him [Douglass' master] three dollars at the end of each week, and to board and clothe myself, and buy my own calking [sic] tools."[41] Self-hire, Douglass noted, was "another step in my career toward freedom."[42]

Not every self-hire slave fared so well. Some were offered the prospect of buying themselves only to see the terms of the contract change. Slaves who earned larger sums than originally expected were required to pay the extra money to the master. Sometimes slaves who made agreements with their masters to pay a certain price for their freedom were sold shortly before the final payment was due.

So intense was the drive to earn money that some slaves were willing to work all day in the fields, then steal away under cover of darkness to work for wages, returning to the fields the next morning. Catahoula Parish (Louisiana) plantation owner John Liddell sought legal action, telling his lawyer, "I request that you would forthwith proceed to prosecute *John S. Sullivan* of Troy, Parish of Catahoula, for Hiring four of my Negro men, secretly, and without my knowledge or permission, at *midnight* on the 12th of August last 1849 (or between midnight and day)."[43]

So common was the practice of self-hire that historians have described the people so employed as "Quasi-Free Negroes" or "Slaves Without Masters."[44] In 1802, a French visitor to New Orleans noticed "a great many loose negroes about."[45] Officials in Savannah, Mobile, Charleston, and other cities talked about "nominal slaves," "quasi f.n. [free Negroes]," and "virtually free negroes," who were seemingly oblivious to any law or regulation.[46] In the Upper South—Baltimore, Washington, Norfolk, Louisville, Richmond, and Lexington, Virginia, for example—large numbers of quasi-free slaves contracted with white builders as skilled carpenters, coopers, and mechanics, while the less skilled worked as servants, hack drivers, and barbers. The quasi-free individuals, more entrepreneurial, established market stalls where they traded fish, produce, and other goods with plantation slaves and sold various commodities to whites. Historian Ira Berlin said, in describing the pre-staple crop period in the Low Country of South Carolina, "The autonomy of the isolated cow pen and the freedom of movement of stock raising allowed made a mockery of the total dominance that chattel bondage implied."[47]

William Rosoe operated a small pleasure boat on the Chesapeake Bay. Ned Hyman, a North Carolina slave, amassed an estate "consisting of Lands chiefly, Live Stock, Negroes and money worth between $5,000 and $6,000 listed in his free Negro wife's name." Whites in his neighborhood said "he was a remarkable, uncommon Negro" and was "remarkably industrious, frugal & prudent. . . . In a word, his character as fair and as good—for honesty, truth, industry, humility, sobriety & fidelity—as any they (your memoralists) have ever seen or hear of."[48]

Thomas David, a slave, owned a construction business in Bennettsville, South Carolina, where he built houses as well as "several larger buildings." He hired laborers, many of whom were slaves themselves, and taught them the necessary skills. This practice of slaves entering the market and competing successfully with whites became so prevalent that a group of the latter in New Hanover County, North Carolina, petitioned the state legislature to ban the practice. But despite statutes to the contrary, slaves continued to work as mechanics (as such workers were then called), contracting on their own "sometimes less than one half the rate that a regular bred white Mechanic could afford to do it."[49]

In Tennessee, it was illegal for a slave to practice medicine; however, "Doctor Jack" did so with "great & unparalleled success," even though he was forced to give a sizable portion of his earnings to his owner, William Macon. After Macon died, Doctor Jack set up his practice in Nashville. Patients thought so much of his services that they appealed to the state legislature: "The undersigned citizens of Tennessee respectfully petition the Honourable Legislature of the State to repeal, amend or so modify the Act of 1831, chap. 103, S[ect]. 3, which prohibits Slaves from practicing medicine, as to exempt from its operation a Slave named Jack. . . ."[50]

Women were also found among slave entrepreneurs. They established stalls and small stores selling various products. They managed modest businesses as seamstresses, laundresses, and weavers. A Maryland slave recalled, "After my father was sold, my master gave my mother permission to work for herself, provided she gave him one half [of the profits]."[51] She ran two businesses, a coffee shop at an army garrison, and a secondhand store selling trousers, shoes, caps, and other items. Despite protests by poor whites, she "made quite a respectable living."[52]

With the increasing number of self-hire and quasi-free blacks came many complaints and attempts at restricting their economic activities. In 1826, Georgia prohibited blacks from trading "any quantity or amount whatever of cotton, tobacco, wheat, rye, oats, corn, rice or poultry or any other articles, except such as are known to be usually manufactured or vended by slaves."[53] Tennessee applied similar restrictions to livestock. Virginia enacted legislation whereby an individual who bought or received any commodity from a slave would be given thirty-nine lashes "well laid on" or fined four times the value of the commodity.

Similar measures were enacted elsewhere. In addition to statutes against trading with slaves, there were laws governing master-slave relationships. North Carolina decreed in 1831 that a master who allowed a slave to "go at large as a freeman, exercising his or her own discre[t]ion in the employment of his or her time . . . shall be fined in the discretion of the court."[54] In 1835, the North Carolina General Assembly enacted a measure "for the better regulation of the slave labourers in the town and Port of Wilmington. . . . That if any slave shall hereafter be permitted to go at large, and make his own contracts to work, and labour in said town, by consent, and with the knowledge of his or her owner or master, the owner of the said slave shall forfeit and pay one hundred dollars . . . said slave shall receive such punishment as said commissioners or town magistrate shall think proper to direct to be inflicted, not exceeding twenty-five lashes."[55]

Similar statutes were enacted in most slave states. In the 1830s, a South Carolina court of appeals ruled as follows: "if the owner without a formal act of emancipation permit his slave to go at large and to exercise all the rights and enjoy all the privileges of a free person of color, the slave becomes liable to seizure as a derelict."[56]

A New Orleans newspaper, the *Daily Picayune,* complained that hired-out slaves had the liberty "to engage in business on their own account, to live according to the suggestions of their own fancy, to be idle or industrious, as the inclination for one or the other prevailed, provided only the monthly wages are regularly gained."[57] In 1855, Memphis' *Daily Appeal* demanded the strengthening of an ordinance prohibiting slaves from hiring themselves out without a permit. One citizen complained that "to permit the negro to hire his own time sends a slave to ruin as property, debauches a slave, and makes him a strolling agent of discontent, disorder, and immorality among our slave population."[58]

Much of the restrictive legislation was prompted or justified by the charge that some slaves were trafficking in stolen goods. But there was also concern that the self-hired and quasi-free would undermine the slavery system itself by breeding discontent and rebellion among slaves in general. Despite all the legal prohibitions, the self-hire and quasi-free practices prospered and expanded. Some slave owners who had sired children felt that, although they might not set those offspring free, they would allow them to be quasi-free and to own property. Other owners considered it simply sound policy to permit slaves a degree of freedom as a reward for good work. Even owners with a strong ideological commitment to the institution of slavery found it profitable to permit self-hire, particularly for their most talented and trusted bondsmen.

By the 1840s and '50s, many masters were earning good returns on slaves who found employment in Baltimore, Nashville, St. Louis, Savannah, Charleston, and New Orleans.[59] In 1856, white builders in Smithfield, North Carolina, complained that they were being underbid by quasi-free blacks in the construction of houses and boats, and criticized white contractors who pursued such hiring practices. Whites in the Sumter District of South Carolina protested that "The law in relation to Slaves hiring their own time is not enforced with sufficient promptness and efficiency as to accomplish the object designed by its enactment."[60]

The fact that self-hire became such a large part of slavery simply reflects the economics of the matter. Faced with fluctuating demands for the labor of slaves, it sometimes made sense for owners to let a slave hire himself out rather than to sit idle, in return for securing a portion of his outside earnings. Slaves favored hiring out because it gave them a measure of freedom; it also provided some income to purchase goods that would be otherwise unattainable.

Free Blacks in the North

Free blacks played a significant economic role in northern cities. In 1838, a pamphlet titled "A Register of Trades of Colored People in the City of Philadelphia and Districts" listed fifty-seven different occupations totaling 656 persons: bakers (eight), blacksmiths (twenty-three), brass founders (three), cabinetmakers and carpenters (fifteen), confectioners (five), and tanners (thirty-one). Black females engaged in businesses were also included in the register: dressmakers and tailoresses (eighty-one), dyers and scourers (four), and cloth fullers and glass/papermakers (two each).[61]

Philadelphia was home to several very prosperous black businesses. Stephen Smith and William Whipper had one of the largest wood and coal yards in the city. As an example of the size of their business, they had, in 1849, "several thousand bushels of coal, 250,000 feet of lumber, 22 merchantmen cars running between Philadelphia and Baltimore, and $9,000 worth of stock in the Columbia bridge." At his death, Smith left an estate worth $150,000; he had earlier given an equal amount to establish the Home for the Aged and Infirm Colored Persons in Philadelphia and had also donated the ground for the Mount Olive Cemetery for Colored People.[62]

Another prosperous enterprise among early Philadelphia blacks was sail-making. Nineteen black sail-making businesses were recorded in the 1838 *Register*. James Forten (1766–1841), the most prominent of them, employed forty black and white workers in his factory in 1829. Stephen Smith was another black entrepreneur, a lumber merchant who was grossing $100,000 annually in sales by the 1850s. By 1854, Smith's net worth was estimated at $500,000, earning him a credit entry as the "King of the Darkies w. 100m. [with $100,000]"[63]

Blacks dominated Philadelphia's catering business. Peter Augustine and Thomas Dorsey were the most prominent among them. Both men earned worldwide fame for their art, with Augustine often sending his terrapin as far away as Paris.[64] Robert Bogle was a waiter who conceived of the catering idea in Philadelphia by contracting formal dinners for those who entertained in their homes. Nicolas Biddle, a leading Philadelphia financier and president of the Bank of United States, honored him by writing an "Ode to Ogle [sic]."[65] Philadelphia blacks ". . . owned fifteen meeting houses and burial grounds adjacent, and one public hall." Their real estate holdings were estimated at $600,000 ($12 million today) and their personal property at more than $677,000."[66] Henry and Sarah Gordon, two other black caterers, became so prosperous that they were able to contribute $66,000 to the Home for the Aged and Infirm Colored Persons.[67]

Blacks made their business presence felt in other northern cities as well. In 1769, ex-slave Emmanuel established Providence, Rhode Island's first oyster-and-ale house. In New York, Thomas Downing operated a successful restaurant to serve his Wall Street clientele before facing competition from two other blacks, George Bell and George Alexander, who opened similar establishments nearby.[68] In 1865, Boston's leading catering establishment was owned and operated by a black. Thomas Dalton, also of Boston, was the proprietor of a prosperous clothing store valued at a half-million dollars at the time of his death. John Jones of Chicago, who owned one of the city's leading tailoring establishments, left behind a fortune of $100,000.[69]

Most blacks of course labored at low-skilled tasks. They nonetheless encountered opposition from whites. When the two races competed, or threatened to do so, violence often resulted. A commission looking into the causes of the 1834 Philadelphia riot, concluded as follows:

> An opinion prevails, especially among white laborers, that certain portions of our community, prefer to employ colored people, whenever they can be had, to the employing of white people; and in consequence of this preference, many whites, who are able and willing to work, are left

without employment, while colored people are provided with work, and enabled comfortably to maintain their families; thus many white laborers, anxious for employment, are kept idle and indigent. Whoever mixed in the crowds and groups, at the late riots, must so often have heard those complaints, as to convince them, that . . . they . . . stimulated many of the most active among the rioters.[70]

Racism and the fear of similar violence prompted New York City authorities to refuse licenses to black carmen and porters, warning, "it would bring them into collision with white men of the same calling, and they would get their horses and carts 'dumped' into the dock and themselves abused and beaten."[71]

The growth of the black labor force, augmented by emancipated and fugitive slaves, also contributed to white fears of black competition. In 1834, a group of Connecticut petitioners declared:

The white man cannot labor upon equal terms with the negro. Those who have just emerged from the state of barbarism or slavery have few artificial wants. Regardless of the decencies of life, and improvement of the future, the black can afford to offer his services at lower prices than the white man.[72]

The petitioners warned the legislature that if entry restrictions were not adopted, the (white) sons of Connecticut would be soon driven from the state by black porters, truckmen, sawyers, mechanics, and laborers of every description.

For their part, blacks soon faced increased competition from the nearly five million Irish, German, and Scandinavian immigrants who reached our shores between 1830 and 1860. Poverty-stricken Irish crowded into shantytowns and sought any kind of employment, regardless of pay and work conditions. One black observer wrote:

These impoverished and destitute beings, transported from transatlantic shores are crowding themselves into every place of business and of labor, and driving the poor colored American citizen out. Along the wharves, where the colored man once done the whole business of shipping and unshipping—in stores where his services were once rendered, and in families where the chief places were filled by him, in all these situations there are substituted foreigners or white Americans.[73]

Irish immigrants did not immediately replace black workers, because employers initially preferred black "humility" to Irish "turbulence." "Help Wanted" ads often read like this one in the *New York Herald* of May 13, 1853: "A Cook, Washer and Ironer: who perfectly understands her business; any color or country except Irish."[74] The *New York Daily Sun* (May 11, 1853) carried: "Woman Wanted—To do general housework . . . English, Scotch, Welsh, German, or any country or color will answer except Irish." The *New York Daily Tribune,* on May 14, 1852, advertised: "Coachman Wanted—A Man who understands the care of horses and is willing to make himself generally useful, on a small place six miles from the city. A colored man preferred. No Irish need apply."[75]

Indicative of racial preferences was the fact that, in 1853, black waiters *in New York* earned *more* than their white counterparts: $16 per month compared to $12. To increase their bargaining power and to dupe their white counterparts out of jobs, black waiters tricked them into striking for *$18* a day. When the strike ended, only the best white waiters were retained; the rest were replaced by blacks.[76]

The mid-nineteenth century saw the early growth of the labor union movement. As I will discuss in more detail in a later chapter, the new unions directed considerable hostility at blacks and often excluded them from membership. When New York longshoremen struck in 1855 against wage cuts, black workers replaced them and violent clashes ensued. The *Frederick Douglass Paper* expressed little sympathy for white strikers: "[C]olored men can feel no obligation to hold out in a 'strike' with the whites, as the latter have never recognized them."[77]

Abolitionist William Lloyd Garrison and many of his followers had similarly little sympathy with white attempts to form labor unions. They felt that employer desire for profit would override racial preferences. Garrison declared, "Place two mechanics by the side of each other, one colored and one white, he who works the cheapest and the best will get the most custom. In making a bargain, the color of the man will never be consulted."[78] Demonstrating an economic understanding that's lost on many of today's black advocates, abolitionists urged blacks to underbid white workers rather than to combine with them. *New England Magazine* remarked:

> After all the voice of interest is louder, and speaks more to the purpose, than reason or philanthropy. When a black merchant shall sell his goods cheaper than his white neighbor, he will have the most customers. . . . When a black mechanic shall work cheaper and better than a white one, he will be more frequently employed.[79]

During this period, black leadership exhibited a vision not often observed today, namely, lowering the price of goods or services is one of the most effective tools to compete. At a black convention in 1848, it was declared, "To be dependent is to be degraded. Men may pity us, but they cannot respect us." Black conventions repeatedly called upon blacks to learn agricultural and mechanical pursuits, to form joint-stock companies, mutual savings banks, and county associations in order to pool resources to purchase land and capital. In 1853, Frederick Douglass warned, "Learn trades or starve!"[80]

Many blacks absorbed the lessons of competition. Virginia's Robert Gordon sold slack (fine screenings of coal) from his white father's coal yard, making what was then a small fortune of $15,000. By 1846, Gordon had purchased his freedom and moved to Cincinnati, where he invested those earnings in a coal yard and built a private dock on the waterfront. White competitors tried to run him out of business through ruthless price-cutting. Gordon cleverly responded by hiring fair-complexioned mulattos to purchase coal from price-cutting competitors, then used that coal to fill his own customers' orders.[81] Gordon retired in 1865, invested his profits in real estate, and eventually passed his fortune to his daughter.

While still a slave, Frank McWorter set up a saltpeter factory in Kentucky's Pulaski County at the start of the War of 1812. After the war, he expanded his factory to meet the growing demand for gunpowder by westward-bound settlers. As a result of his enterprise, McWorter purchased his wife's freedom in 1817 and his own in 1819 for a total cost of $1,600.[82]

Born a slave in Kentucky, Junius G. Graves went to Kansas in 1879. He worked on a farm for forty cents a day and by 1884 had amassed the sum of $2,200. Six years later, he owned 500 acres of land valued at $100,000.

"Because of his success in producing a-greater-than-average-yield of pota-toes per acre and because of his being the largest individual grower of potatoes, he was called 'The Negro Potato King.'"[83]

Other examples of nineteenth-century black enterprise abound: William W. Browne founded the first black bank in Virginia; H. C. Haynes invented the Haynes Razor Strop in Chicago; A. C. Howard manufactured shoe polish (7,200 boxes per day) in Chicago.[84]

Licensing as a Strategy of Exclusion

As the Civil War approached, New Orleans' attitude toward free blacks changed with restrictions on the kind of businesses they could enter, along with licensure laws and an increasing hostile press. Some blacks saw migra-tion as an alternative to the harassment. Haiti's emperor sent an agent to New Orleans to encourage them to take that option, and at least 281 "lit-erate and respectable" free blacks migrated between 1859–1860. Said the *Daily Picayune,* the most rabid of New Orleans' race-baiting newspapers:

> They [free Negroes] form the great majority of our regular settled masons, bricklayers, builders, carpenters, tailors, shoemakers etc., whose sudden emigration from this community would certainly be attended with some degree of annoyance; whilst we can count among them no small number of excellent musicians, jewelers, goldsmiths, tradesmen and merchants.[85]

The newspaper went on to add that this population constituted a sober, industrious, and moral class, far advanced in education and civilization.

New Orleans was not the only city to enact licensure laws restricting economic activity of free blacks. A Washington, D.C., ordinance enacted in 1836 said:

> It shall not be lawful for the mayor to grant a license, for any purpose whatever, to any free negro or mulatto, except licenses to drive carts, drays, hackney carriages, or wagons.

The ordinance also prohibited licenses for blacks to operate taverns, restaurants, or any other eating establishment and from selling alcoholic beverages. A free black, Isaac N. Carey, who had been fined $50 for selling perfumery without a license, brought suit in the D.C. Circuit Court. In reversing the judgment against Carey, Chief Judge William Cranch said:

> It is said that colored persons are a distinct class, not entitled to equal rights with whites, and may be prohibited although whites may not. . . . Although free colored persons have not the same political rights which are enjoyed by free white persons, yet they have the same civil right, except so far as they are abridged by the general law of the land. Among these civil rights is the right to exercise any lawful and harmless trade, business, or occupation.[86]

Two years later, the same court held that the Corporation of D.C. did have "a discretion to prohibit the granting of tavern licenses to colored persons."[87]

During this early period, blacks came to dominate the very lucrative hackney business in the nation's capital. One visitor called the city "the very paradise of hackney coachmen," adding, "If these men do not get rich it must be owing to some culpable extravagance for their vehicles [which] are in continuous demand from the hour of dinner until five in the morning, and long distances and heavy charges are all in their favor."[88]

In addition to black hackney owners, there were black barbers, restaurant owners, waiters, teachers, preachers, and skilled workers. Blacks became significant landowners in the district, paying taxes on over $600,000 worth of property on the eve of the Civil War. Two examples of black business success: James Wormley, who became proprietor of the famous Wormley Hotel; Alfred Jones and Alfred Lee, who made very good money as feed dealers.[89]

Summary

This brief historical overview has aimed simply to highlight several important principles that will be discussed in subsequent chapters. Gross racial discrimination alone has never been sufficient to prevent blacks from earning a living and bettering themselves by working as skilled or unskilled craftsmen and as business owners, accumulating considerable wealth. The fact that whites sought out blacks as artisans and workers, while patronizing black businesses, can hardly be said to be a result of white enlightenment. A far better explanation: market forces at work.

The relative color blindness of the market accounts for much of the hostility towards it. Markets have a notorious lack of respect for privilege, race, and class structures. White customers patronized black-owned businesses because their prices were lower or their product quality or service better. Whites hired black skilled and unskilled labor because their wages were lower or they made superior employees.

People have always sought to use laws to accomplish what they cannot accomplish through voluntary, peaceable exchange. As will be argued in subsequent chapters, restrictive laws harm blacks equally, whether they were written with the explicit intent — as in the past — to eliminate black competition or written — as in our time — with such benign goals as protecting public health, safety and welfare, and preventing exploitation of workers.

CHAPTER 3

Race and Wage Regulation

Of sentences that stir my bile,
Of phrases I detest,
There's one beyond all others vile:
"He did it for the best."
—James Kenneth Stephen, *The Malefactor's Plea*

SOME MIGHT FIND IT PUZZLING that during the times of gross racial discrimination, black unemployment was lower and blacks were more active in the labor market than they are today. In 1910, for example, 71 percent of blacks over nine years of age were employed, compared to 51 percent for whites.[1] Earlier periods display the same pattern. Table 3.1 shows the employment-to-population ratio by race between 1900 and 1990. After 1930, however, the nonwhite employment-population ratio fell significantly, while the white ratio rose significantly. Also during earlier periods, the duration of unemployment among blacks was shorter than among white—between 1890 and 1900, by 13 percent; in more recent times, the duration for blacks has been 15 percent *longer* than for whites.[2]

In the early 1900s, coal mining companies competed vigorously for black workers.[3] Robert Higgs shows a high percentage (87.4) of blacks gainfully employed in 1910.[4] Moreover, during these earlier periods, the black wage rate for agricultural employment was nearly identical to that of whites.[5] In 1908, a keen observer of the South, Ray Stannard Baker, said, "One of the most significant things I saw in the South—and I saw it

Table 3.1. The Employment–Population Ratio by Race in the United States, 1900 to 1990

Year	% Employment– Population Ratio: Nonwhites	% Employment– Population Ratio: Whites	Nonwhite to White Employment–Population Ratio
1900	57.4	45.5	1.26 to 1
1930	60.2	44.7	1.35 to 1
1954	58.0	55.2	1.50 to 1
1975	50.1	56.7	0.88 to 1
1990	56.2	63.6	0.88 to 1

Source: Richard K. Vedder and Lowell E. Galloway, *Out of Work: Unemployment and Government in Twentieth-Century America* (New York: Holmes & Meir, 1993), 281.

everywhere—was the way in which the white people were torn between their feeling of racial prejudice and their downright economic needs."[6]

Those observations cannot be explained simply by racial tastes. Surely, one cannot explain the fact of higher black employment rates during earlier periods as a product of less racial discrimination. Competition and open markets, unhampered by government sanctions and subsidies for race discrimination, provide a far better explanation for why blacks had a much greater labor-force participation rate and a lower unemployment rate than that of whites during a particularly racially hostile period in U.S. history. Richard Vedder and Lowell Galloway suggest that while other factors may have been at work, New Deal interventions (Davis-Bacon Act, Fair Labor Standards Act, National Labor Relations Act, Social Security Act, and other labor legislation) during the 1930s and later cannot be easily dismissed as a major factor in reducing work opportunities for blacks.

The Davis-Bacon Act

Kansas, in 1891, was the first state to establish what has become known as prevailing wage laws.[7] The law read: "That not less than the current rate of per diem wages in the locality where the work is performed shall be paid to laborers, workmen, mechanics and other persons so employed by or on behalf of the state of Kansas. . . ."[8] In 1894, New York became the second state to enact a prevailing wage law. Samuel Gompers, president of the American Federation of Labor (AFL), led the political charge in both states and later the call for a federal prevailing wage law.

The impetus for a law at the federal level began in 1927, when an Alabama contractor successfully won a bid on a government contract to build a Veterans Bureau hospital on Long Island. Ethelbert Stewart, commissioner of labor statistics, said, "A contractor from a Southern State secured a contract to build a Government marine hospital, as I remember it, on Long Island; . . . he brought with him an entire outfit of Negro laborers from the South. . . ."[9] In response to the Alabama contractor's underbidding of his local counterparts, New York Representative Robert Bacon submitted H.R. 17069, "A Bill to Require Contractors and Subcontractors Engaged on Public Works of the United States to Comply with State Laws Relating to Hours of Labor and Wages of Employees on State Public Works."

Between 1927 and 1930, Congress introduced at least fourteen bills to regulate wages on public works projects.[10] And as the Depression deepened, Congress's unwillingness to interfere with *private* employment contracts changed. By 1931, construction industry wages had fallen by one-half, and 700,000 construction workers became unemployed as construction projects fell by 70 percent between 1929 and 1933.[11] Congressmen received numerous complaints that contractors were bidding wages down and employing itinerants to replace local workers. That wave of unemployment, together with resulting complaints, ultimately strengthened the hand of unions pressing for the enactment of a prevailing wage law at the federal level.

In support of Representative Bacon's bill, Representative William Upshaw of Georgia complained of the "superabundance or large aggregation of negro labor," which he characterized as a problem "you are confronted with in any community."[12] In response to Bacon's description of his district hospital's situation, Upshaw remarked: "You will not think a southern man is more than human if he smiles over the fact of your reaction to the real problem you are confronted with in any community with a superabundance or aggregation of Negro labor."[13] To which Bacon replied: "I just mentioned the fact because that was the fact in this particular case, but the same would be true if you should bring in a lot of Mexican laborers or if you brought in *any non-union laborers* from any other state."[14]

Finally, after thirteen additional, similar bills had been submitted, one, co-sponsored by Representative Bacon and Pennsylvania Senator James J. Davis passed on March 31, 1931. It mandated the payment of locally prevailing wages and benefits on all federally financed, or assisted, construction projects that exceeded $5,000 (reduced to $2,000 four years later). The Davis-Bacon Act had established federally mandated super-minimum wages in the construction industry.

While blacks were excluded from most major construction unions, they were nonetheless a formidable force in the construction industry. In 1930, the industry in the South provided more jobs to blacks than any other except agriculture and domestic services.[15] In six Southern cities, blacks represented more than 80 percent of the unskilled labor force.[16] They were also represented among skilled construction workers, for example, comprising 17 percent of carpenters. During this period, significant demographic changes were taking place. Blacks were increasingly migrating northward and establishing a foothold in the Northern construction workforce.[17]

As can be seen from the congressional testimony of its supporters, the Davis-Bacon Act was aimed at decoupling that foothold. Said Representative Clayton Allgood, "Reference has been made to a contractor from Alabama who went to New York with bootleg labor. This is a fact. That contractor has cheap colored labor that he transports, and he puts them in cabins, and it is labor of that sort that is in competition with white labor throughout the country. This bill has merit, and with the extensive building program now being entered into, it is very important that we enact this measure."[18] Representative John J. Cochran of Missouri voiced similar sentiments, saying he had "received numerous complaints in recent months about Southern contractors employing low-paid colored mechanics getting work and bringing the employees from the South."[19] William Green, president of the American Federation of Labor, made clear the unions' interests: "[C]olored labor is being sought to demoralize wage rates [in Tennessee]."[20]

In addition to black workers, those of non-European descent were targeted. In 1927, Representative Bacon entered in the *Congressional Record* a statement by thirty-four university professors concerning the new immigration law: "We urge the extension of the quota system to all countries of North and South America from which we have substantial migration and in which the population is not predominantly of the white race. . . . Only by this method can that large proportion of our population which is descended from the colonists . . . have their proper racial representation. . . .

Congress wisely concluded that only by such a system of proportional representation . . . could the racial status quo be maintained."[21]

Bacon's reference was to the Johnson Act of 1924, which established immigration quotas. Representative Anning Prall said, "On this job [Fort Wadsworth Reservation] secured by a private contractor, 50 percent of the carpenters employed at one time were aliens, while thousands of unemployed American citizens were tramping the streets looking for work."[22] Representative Hamilton Fish said, in support of the Davis-Bacon Act, "In conclusion I want to say that I am wholeheartedly for the bill. I do not think it goes far enough. I'm sorry there is not a clause in the bill to give preference to local and American labor over alien labor."[23] Added Representative Fiorello La Guardia of New York, "The workmanship of the cheap imported labor was of course very inferior."[24] Other congressmen testifying in support of Davis-Bacon lamented the use of "cheap labor," "migratory labor," and "minimum labor" underbidding American workers.[25]

Effects of the Davis-Bacon Act

Davis-Bacon exemplifies collusion between a seller (labor) and contractors (buyers) on federal construction projects to insure payment to workers of a minimum ("prevailing") wage. The Secretary of Labor determines the prevailing wage according to various formulas. One study found that over 90 percent of the determinations equaled the union rate in the area, although non-union work accounted for large fractions of construction workers. Another study showed that Davis-Bacon determinations are 4 percent higher than average wages in commercial construction and 9 percent higher in residential construction.[26] A more recent survey found that Davis-Bacon wage determinations were 15 to 40 percent higher than market wages. For example, Davis-Bacon wages for a carpenter in New York ranged between $34 and $40, while the market wage was around $24.[27]

In practice, and contrary to the Davis-Bacon Act, prevailing wages are determined by the Department of Labor to be the union wage in the area or higher, and "therefore have been useful to the building trades union in preventing minimum wage competition below these minimums."[28] The act's wage and work jurisdiction requirements make it costly for non-union shops to hire and train unskilled workers, because they had to pay workers wages and benefits that exceed worker productivity. Initially, the act's regulations did not make a distinction between unskilled and skilled workers unless the former were members of a union apprenticeship program. As a result, contractors were forced to pay a worker who was not a member of such a program the same wage as a skilled worker.

Given that situation, Ralph C. Thomas, executive director of the National Association of Minority Contractors, said that a contractor has "no choice but to hire skilled tradesmen, the majority of which are majority [white]. . . . Davis-Bacon . . . closes the door in such activity in an industry most capable of employing the largest numbers of minorities."[29] Government paperwork requirements, to be in compliance with the Davis-Bacon Act, have a differential adverse impact on small, non-union contractors. Unlike major contractors, small ones typically do not have attorneys on retainer and/or personnel with the expertise necessary for paperwork compliance. This confers a competitive advantage on larger, usually unionized, contractors who do have such resources.[30]

According to Vedder and Galloway, prior to the enactment of the Davis-Bacon Act, black and white construction unemployment registered similar levels. After the enactment of the Davis-Bacon Act, however, black unemployment rose relative to that of whites.[31] Vedder and Galloway also argue that 1930 to 1950 was a period of unprecedented and rapidly increasing government intervention in the economy. This period saw enactment of the bulk of legislation restraining the setting of private wage, such as the Fair Labor Standards Act, Davis-Bacon Act, Walsh-Healey Act, and National Labor Relations Act. The Social Security Act also played a role, forcing employers to pay for a newly imposed fringe benefit.[32] Vedder and Galloway also note that this period saw a rapid increase in the black/white unemployment ratio.

Cases of Davis-Bacon Exclusion

The U.S. Department of Housing and Urban Development (HUD) finances housing rehabilitation programs. Since they are federally funded, the programs come under the jurisdiction of the Davis-Bacon Act. Mary Nelson, director of Bethel New Life Inc., a Chicago-based social service organization, found that Davis-Bacon adds as much as 25 percent to her housing renovation costs. It frequently prevents her from hiring the low-income, low-skills residents to do rehabilitation work in the housing project in which they live.[33]

Elzie Higginbottom builds low-income housing in Chicago. In order to comply with the provisions of Davis-Bacon, he must pay carpenters (defined by the Labor Department as anyone who hammers a nail) $23 an hour. Higginbottom says, "I've got to start out a guy at $16 an hour to find out if he knows how to dig a hole. I can't do that." As a result he is prevented from hiring unskilled local blacks.[34]

Ralph L. Jones is the president of a company that manages housing projects for HUD. When Jones decided to repair 200 dilapidated units, he planned to employ unskilled residents, at $5 an hour, to pull out unsalvageable parts of the building and later to assist skilled craftsmen in restoring the property. However, the Davis-Bacon Act required that he pay laborers $14 an hour. He was forced to hire only skilled laborers, very few of whom were black or residents of the project.[35]

Constitutional Test of the Davis-Bacon Act

On November 9, 1993, the Washington-based Institute for Justice filed a lawsuit challenging the constitutionality of the Davis-Bacon Act. The case is *Brazier Construction Co., et al. v. Robert Reich, et al.* The plaintiffs were four black construction contractors and three public housing tenant organizations. They argued that, according to previous Supreme Court decisions, a statute may have discriminatory purpose even if it is neither "expressed [in] or appear[s] on the face of the statute."[36] In fact, courts may "[d]etermine whether invidious discriminatory purpose was a motivating factor" by conducting "a sensible inquiry into such circumstantial and direct evidence as may be available."[37] According to its decision in *Village of Arlington Heights v. Metropolitan Housing Development Corporation,* the Supreme Court held that for a statute to be constitutionally invalid, racial discrimination does not have to be the sole motivating factor but only one motivating factor.[38] When the legislative intent of the statute can be reasonably shown to be racially discriminatory, judicial deference to the legislature is not justified. The court has held that "the legislative or administrative history may be highly relevant, especially where there are contemporary statements by members of the decision-making body, minutes of its meetings, or reports" among the factors that can be used to prove racially discriminatory intent.

In 2002, the U.S. District Court for the District of Columbia ruled against the plaintiffs. The decision was not appealed.

Minimum Wages

The minimum wage law has a history that started well before it became a federal law. In September 1918, the District of Columbia Wage Board enacted a law providing for the fixing of minimum wages for women and children. In 1923, the law was challenged in the U.S. Supreme Court in *Adkins v. Children's Hospital*[39] and was eventually held unconstitutional by a 5–3 decision. The constitutionality of the minimum wage law made its way into the Supreme Court again in 1937 in *West Coast Hotel v. Parrish*. By a 5–4 vote, the court reversed its earlier ruling and upheld the validity of the Washington State statute.[40] That paved the way for the Fair Labor Standards Act (FLSA) of 1938, establishing a federal minimum wage law that applies to employees engaged in and producing goods for interstate commerce.

The FLSA enacted by Congress has been amended many times to increase the legal minimums and the extent of employment coverage under its provisions. Initially, workers exempt from coverage of the act included agricultural and seasonal laborers, handlers of perishable goods, and workers in certain industries covered by collective bargaining. Recently enacted legislation has created a three-step increase in the federal hourly minimum wage: $5.85 in 2007, $6.55 in 2008, and $7.25 in 2009. The federal minimum wage is complemented by state laws that sometimes exceed the federal requirements. Federal and state minimum wage laws represent deliberate governmental intervention in the labor market to produce a pattern of results other than that produced in a free labor market.

Minimum Wage Effects

Understanding the effects of minimum wage laws requires first a few simple observations. While legislative bodies have the power to order wage increases, they have not found a way to order commensurate increases in worker productivity that make the worker's output worth the higher wage.

Further, while Congress can legislate the wage at which labor transactions occur, it cannot require that the transaction actually be made. That is, Congress has not yet chosen to mandate that a worker actually be hired. To the extent that the minimum wage law raises a worker's pay level that exceeds his productivity, employers, predictably, make adjustments in their use of labor.[41] Such an adjustment will produce gains for some workers at the expense of other workers. Those workers who retain their jobs receive a higher wage gain. Most of the adverse effects are borne by the workers who are most disadvantaged in terms of marketable skills. They will lose their jobs or not be hired in the first place.

The effect of the minimum wage law is more clearly seen if we put ourselves in the place of an employer and ask: if a wage of $7.25 per hour must be paid no matter who is hired, what kind of worker does it pay to hire?[42] Clearly the answer, in terms of profit and economic efficiency, is to hire one whose productivity equals or exceeds $7.25 per hour. If such workers are available, it does not pay the firm to hire those whose productive output is, say, worth only $4 per hour. Even if an employer were willing to train such a worker, the fact that he must be paid a wage higher than the market value of his output makes on-the-job training an unattractive proposition.

The impact of legislated minimums can be brought into sharper focus if we ask a distributional question: who bears the burden of the minimum wage? As suggested earlier, it is the workers who are the most marginal, that is, those who employers perceive as being less productive, more costly, or otherwise less desirable to employ than other workers. In the U.S. there are at least two segments of the labor force that share marginal worker characteristics to a greater extent than do other segments of the labor force. The first group consists of youths in general. They are low-skilled or marginal because of their age, immaturity, and lack of work experience. The second group, which contains members of the first, are racial minorities, such as blacks and Hispanics who, as a result of historical factors, are disproportionately represented among low-skilled workers. They are not only made less employable by minimum wages; opportunities to upgrade their skills through on-the-job training are also severely limited when they find it hard to get jobs.[43]

It is precisely these labor market participants who are disproportionately represented among the unemployment statistics. Youth unemployment, even during relatively prosperous times, ranges from two to three times that of the general labor force. And black youth unemployment, nationally for more than a half century, has ranged from two to three times the corresponding rate for whites. Historically, in some metropolitan areas, black youth unemployment has been higher than 60 percent!

The economic effects of minimum wage legislation have been analyzed in numerous statistical studies.[44] While there is a debate over the magnitude of the effects, the weight of research by academic scholars points to the conclusion that unemployment for some population groups is directly related to legal minimum wages and that the unemployment effects of the minimum wage law are felt disproportionately by nonwhites. Indeed, a 1976 survey by the American Economic Association found that 90 percent of its members agreed that increasing the minimum wage increases unemployment among young and unskilled workers.[45] It was followed by another survey, in 1990, that found that 80 percent of economists agreed with this statement: increases in the minimum wage cause unemployment among the youth and low-skilled.[46]

In addition, whenever one wants to find a broad consensus of opinion in any subject, he should investigate what is said in the introductory and intermediate college textbooks on that subject. When he does this in economics, he finds broad agreement that the minimum wage causes unemployment among low-skilled workers.[47] Reports from several government agencies, such as the General Accounting Office,[48] Congressional Budget Office,[49] and the Council of Economic Advisors,[50] reach the same conclusion.

In 1994, David Card and Alan B. Krueger, two Princeton University economists, published a study that challenged conventional economic wisdom about the unemployment effects of minimum wage laws.[51] The authors surveyed 410 fast-food restaurants in New Jersey and eastern Pennsylvania before and after the 1992 increase in New Jersey's minimum wage from $4.25 to $5.05 per hour. They found no indication that the rise in the minimum wage reduced employment. Later their findings were published in a book titled *Myth and Measurement: The New Economics of the Minimum Wage.*[52] Politicians, labor union officials, and other supporters of higher minimum wages greeted the study with glee and seized upon it to make their political case for legislative increases.

But since the Card and Krueger finding challenges basic economic theory—the law of demand that holds that the higher the price of something the less is taken, and vice versa—the study came under instant professional scrutiny and has been thoroughly discredited.

The major challenge came from the Employment Policies Institute, which issued a 1996 report titled, "New Evidence on the Minimum Wage: The Crippling Flaws in the New Jersey Fast Food Study."[53] They found that the employment effects of the New Jersey minimum wage increase were negative and quite consistent with the prevailing wisdom. A follow-up investigation by Professors David Neumark and William Wascher for the National Bureau of Economic Research showed that Card and Krueger collected data incorrectly.[54]

The best data Card and Krueger could have obtained from these restaurants were the numbers of hours worked. However, they did not obtain that data; instead, they conducted telephone interviews. Neumark and Wascher obtained the payroll data from the restaurants the Princeton professors surveyed. When the former pair calculated the numbers, using the identical statistical methodology of Card and Krueger, they found that unemployment in Pennsylvania rose more rapidly than unemployment in New Jersey. A presidential commission reported in 1980 that teenage employment fell 1 to 3 percent for every 10 percent hike in the minimum wage. The difference between Pennsylvania and New Jersey was exactly within that range.[55]

Although most people are familiar with more recent statistics on black youth unemployment, not many are aware of the black/white statistics for earlier periods. Table 3.2 shows that in 1948, the two were roughly equal. For that year, blacks aged sixteen to seventeen had an unemployment rate that was *less* than whites of the same age—9.4 percent compared to a 10.2 percent. During the same period (until the mid-1960s), Table 3.3 shows that black youths generally were either just as active as whites in the labor force or more so. Since the '60s, both the labor-force participation rate and the employment rate of black youths has fallen to what it is today. For those sixteen to seventeen years of age, the participation rate is less than 60 percent of that of white youths. During earlier periods, as shown in Table 3.2, the rate was equal to or higher than that of white youths.

Table 3.2. Comparison of Youth and General Unemployment by Race (Males)

Year	General	White 16–17	Black 16–17	B/W Ratio	White 18–19	Black 18–19	B/W Ratio	White 20–24	Black 20–24	B/W Ratio
1948	3.8	10.2	9.4	0.92	9.4	10.5	1.11	6.4	11.7	1.83
1949	5.9	13.4	15.8	1.18	14.2	17.1	1.20	9.8	15.8	1.61
1950*	5.3	13.4	12.1	0.90	11.7	17.7	1.51	7.7	12.6	1.64
1951	3.3	9.5	8.7	0.92	6.7	9.6	1.43	3.6	6.7	1.86
1952	3.0	10.9	8.0	0.73	7.0	10.0	1.43	4.3	7.9	1.84
1953	2.9	8.9	8.3	0.93	7.1	8.1	1.14	4.5	8.1	1.80
1954	5.5	14.0	13.4	0.96	13.0	14.7	1.13	9.8	16.9	1.72
1955	4.4	12.2	14.8	1.21	10.4	12.9	1.24	7.0	12.4	1.77
1956*	4.1	11.2	15.7	1.40	9.7	14.9	1.54	6.1	12.0	1.97
1957	4.3	11.9	16.3	1.37	11.2	20.0	1.70	7.1	12.7	1.79
1958	6.8	14.9	27.1	1.81	16.5	26.7	1.62	11.7	19.5	1.66
1959	5.5	15.0	22.3	1.48	13.0	27.2	2.09	7.5	16.3	2.17
1960	5.5	14.6	22.7	1.55	13.5	25.1	1.86	8.3	13.1	1.58
1961*	6.7	16.5	31.0	1.89	15.1	23.9	1.58	10.0	15.3	1.53
1962	5.5	15.1	21.9	1.45	12.7	21.8	1.72	8.0	14.6	1.83
1963	5.7	17.8	27.0	1.52	14.2	27.4	1.83	7.8	15.5	1.99
1964	5.2	16.1	25.9	1.61	13.4	23.1	1.72	7.4	12.6	1.70
1965	4.5	14.7	27.1	1.84	11.4	20.2	1.77	5.9	9.3	1.58
1966	3.8	12.5	22.5	1.80	8.9	20.5	2.30	4.1	7.9	1.93
1967*	3.8	12.7	28.9	2.26	9.0	20.1	2.23	4.2	8.0	1.90
1968*	3.6	12.3	26.6	2.16	8.2	19.0	2.31	4.6	8.3	1.80
1969	3.5	12.5	24.7	1.98	7.9	19.0	2.40	4.6	8.4	1.83
1970	4.9	15.7	27.8	1.77	12.0	23.1	1.93	7.8	12.6	1.62
1971	5.9	17.1	33.4	1.95	13.5	26.0	1.93	9.4	16.2	1.72
1972	5.6	16.4	35.1	2.14	12.4	26.2	2.11	8.5	14.7	1.73
1973	4.9	15.1	34.4	2.28	10.0	22.1	2.21	6.5	12.6	1.94
1974*	5.6	16.2	39.0	2.41	11.5	26.6	2.31	7.8	15.4	1.97
1975*	8.1	19.7	45.2	2.29	14.0	30.1	2.15	11.3	23.5	2.08
1976*	7.0	19.7	40.6	2.06	15.5	35.5	2.29	10.9	22.4	2.05
1977	6.8	17.6	38.7	2.20	13.0	36.1	2.78	9.3	21.7	2.33
1978*	6.6	19.4	40.4	2.08	13.0	32.2	2.47	10.0	22.5	2.25
1979*	5.8	16.1	34.4	2.14	12.3	29.6	2.41	7.4	17.0	2.30
1980*	7.1	18.5	37.7	2.04	14.6	33.0	2.26	11.1	22.3	2.01
1981*	7.6	19.9	43.2	2.17	16.4	39.2	2.39	11.6	26.4	2.28
1982	9.7	24.2	52.7	2.18	20.0	47.1	2.36	14.3	31.5	2.20
1983	9.6	22.6	52.2	2.31	18.7	47.3	2.53	13.8	31.4	2.28
1984	7.5	19.7	44.0	2.23	15.0	42.2	2.81	9.8	26.6	2.71
1985	7.2	19.2	42.9	2.19	14.7	40.0	2.72	9.7	23.5	2.42

Table 3.2. (*continued*)

Year	General	White 16–17	Black 16–17	B/W Ratio	White 18–19	Black 18–19	B/W Ratio	White 20–24	Black 20–24	B/W Ratio
1986	7.0	18.4	41.4	2.25	14.7	38.2	2.60	9.2	23.5	2.55
1987	6.2	17.9	39.0	2.18	13.7	31.6	2.31	8.4	20.3	2.42
1988	5.5	16.1	34.4	2.14	12.4	31.7	2.56	7.4	19.4	2.62
1989	5.3	16.4	34.4	2.10	12.0	30.3	2.53	7.5	17.9	2.39
1990*	5.5	15.9	38.9	2.44	13.1	28.2	2.15	7.6	20.2	2.66
1991*	6.7	19.4	39.0	2.01	16.3	35.2	2.16	10.2	22.4	2.20
1992	7.4	21.3	47.5	2.23	16.4	39.1	2.38	10.4	24.5	2.36
1993	6.8	20.1	42.7	2.12	15.9	38.6	2.43	9.5	23.0	2.42
1994	6.1	18.5	39.3	2.12	14.7	36.5	2.48	8.8	19.4	2.20

Year	General	White 16–19	Black 16–19	B/W Ratio	White 20–over	Black 20–over	B/W Ratio
1995**	5.2	16.1	38.9	2.42	4.2	9.0	2.14
1996*	5.0	14.7	38.6	2.63	3.8	8.0	2.11
1997*	4.4	10.7	36.7	3.43	3.5	8.2	2.34
1998	4.0	13.7	26.4	1.93	3.2	6.5	2.03
1999	3.7	13.2	25.8	1.95	2.8	6.9	2.46
2000	3.7	12.6	30.8	2.44	3.0	7.2	2.40
2001	5.4	15.3	33.6	2.19	4.7	9.1	1.94
2002	5.7	15.1	36.5	2.41	4.9	10.7	2.18
2003	5.6	16.1	29.6	1.83	5.0	10.4	2.10
2004	5.2	18.0	39.5	2.19	4.6	9.5	2.10
2005	4.7	13.6	23.8	1.75	4.0	10.4	2.60
2006	4.0	14.9	26.9	1.80	3.6	7.6	2.10
2007*	4.1	16.6	39.4	2.40	3.7	7.5	2.00
2008*	6.1	21.5	35.3	1.60	4.9	10.2	2.00
2009*	9.3	27.4	52.2	1.90	8.8	16.3	1.88

*Shows change in the federal minimum wage law.

**After 1994, the Department of Labor no longer reported unemployment by previous age categories.

Sources: Unemployment Rate, by Race and Hispanic Origin: 1980 to 1998, www.census.gov/prod/99pubs/99statab/sec13.pdf (accessed September 29, 2010); Department of Labor, Bureau of Labor Statistics, *The Employment Situation: January 2003, December 2002, 2001, 2000, 1999, 1998, 1997, 1996,* www.bls.gov/schedule/archives/empsit (accessed February 14, 2003); Economagic.com: Economic Time Series Page, *U.S. Labor Force Data from the BLS: Unemployment Rate-Civilian Labor Force 16–19 yes. Black Male;* www.economagic.com/em-cgi/data.exe/BLSLF/LFS21000831 (accessed February 17, 2003); Economagic.com: Economic Time Series Page, *U.S. Labor Force Data from the BLS: Unemployment Rate—Civilian Labor Force 16–19 yrs. White Male;* www.economagic.com/em-cgi/data.exe/BLSLF/LFS21000811 (accessed February 17, 2003); Department of Labor, Bureau of Labor Statistics, data/bls.gov/PDG/servlet/SurveyOutputServlet (accessed February 17, 2003).

Table 3.3. Male Civilian Labor-Force Participation: Ratio by Race and Age

Wage (in dollars)	Year	B/W Males 16–17	B/W Males 18–19	B/W Males 20–24	B/W Males 16 & Over
	1954	0.99	1.11	1.05	1.00
	1955	1.00	1.01	1.05	1.00
1.00/hr.	1956	0.96	1.06	1.01	0.99
	1957	0.95	1.01	1.03	0.99
	1958	0.96	1.03	1.02	1.00
	1959	0.92	1.02	1.04	1.00
	1960	0.99	1.03	1.03	1.00
1.15/hr.	1961	0.96	1.06	1.02	0.99
	1962	0.93	1.04	1.03	0.98
1.25/hr.	1963	0.87	1.02	1.04	0.99
	1964	0.85	1.01	1.04	0.99
	1965	0.88	1.01	1.05	0.99
	1966	0.87	0.97	1.06	0.98
1.40/hr.	1967	0.86	0.95	1.04	0.97
1.60/hr.	1968	0.79	0.96	1.03	0.97
	1969	0.77	0.95	1.02	0.96
	1970	0.71	0.92	1.00	0.96
	1971	0.65	0.87	0.98	0.94
	1972	0.68	0.85	0.97	0.93
	1973	0.63	0.85	0.95	0.93
2.00/hr.	1974	0.65	0.85	0.95	0.92
2.10/hr.	1975	0.57	0.79	0.92	0.91
2.30/hr.	1976	0.57	0.77	0.91	0.90
	1977	0.57	0.77	0.90	0.90
2.65/hr.	1978	0.60	0.79	0.89	0.92
2.90/hr.	1979	0.57	0.78	0.91	0.91
3.10/hr.	1980	0.60	0.76	0.91	0.90
3.35/hr.	1981	0.57	0.75	0.91	0.90
	1982	0.50	0.78	0.91	0.91
	1983	0.53	0.77	0.92	0.92
	1984	0.57	0.79	0.91	0.92
	1985	0.61	0.84	0.91	0.92
	1986	0.62	0.83	0.92	0.93
	1987	0.65	0.81	0.90	0.93
	1988	0.66	0.79	0.92	0.92
	1989	0.66	0.81	0.92	0.92
	1990	0.61	0.74	0.89	0.91
4.25/hr.	1991	0.56	0.72	0.90	0.91
	1992	0.62	0.79	0.88	0.91
	1993	0.61	0.77	0.87	0.90
	1994	0.63	0.78	0.86	0.91

Table 3.3. (*continued*)

Wage (in dollars)	Year	B/W Males 16–19	B/W Males 16–over	B/W Males 20–over
	1995*	0.68	0.94	0.91
4.75/hr.	1996	0.69	0.93	0.90
(5.15)	1997	0.67	0.93	0.90
	1998	0.72	0.93	0.91
	1999	0.68	0.93	0.91
	2000	0.71	0.97	0.95
	2001	0.72	0.98	0.95
	2002	0.64	0.98	0.94
	2003	0.69	0.96	0.93
	2004	0.68	0.97	0.94
	2005	0.71	0.96	0.92
	2006	0.66	0.95	0.91
	2007	0.71	0.97	0.94

*The Bureau of Labor Statistics changed its age-group reporting methods in 1995.

Sources: Computed from the following Department of Labor, Bureau of Labor Statistics publications, all published in Washington by the Government Printing Office: *Handbook of Labor statistics 1975—Reference ed.* (1975) 36–37; *Employment and Unemployment in 1976: Special Labor Force Report 199* (1977)—1978–1980 figures obtained directly from department's Employment Analysis Division; *The Employment Situation: January 2003, December, 2002* (2003), 9,14; *The Employment Situation: 2001* www.bls.census.gov/cps/pub/empsit_jan2001.htm (accessed September 27, 2010).

Faced with those facts, one naturally asks why labor market opportunities have deteriorated so precipitously for black youths. Can racial discrimination explain the reversal? Probably not. It would be very difficult for anyone to argue that employers have now become more racially discriminatory than they were during the 1940s and 1950s. Can we say the lower unemployment for blacks in the past was because they had educational attainment levels and skills equal to or higher than whites? No, we cannot. The answers lie elsewhere. One of those answers is reduced employment opportunities as a result of minimum wage legislation.

But some supporters of the minimum wage law attempt to rebut this line of reasoning with another argument. For example, economist Professor Bernard Anderson said, "The minimum wage argument does not explain why black youths are so disproportionately affected; then why doesn't it reduce it as much for white youths as it does for black youths?"[56] This is not a refutation of economic theory about effects of the minimum wage. It simply suggests that when faced with legislated wages that exceed the productivity of some workers, firms will make adjustments in their use of labor. One adjustment is not only to hire fewer youths but also to seek among them the more highly qualified candidates. It turns out for a number of socioeconomic reasons that white youths, more often than their black counterparts, have higher levels of educational attainment and training.[57] Therefore, a law that discriminates against low-skilled workers can be expected to place a heavier burden on black youths than on white ones.

Employer substitution of higher-skilled for lower-skilled workers is not the only effect of the minimum wage law. It also gives employers an economic incentive to make other changes: substitute machines for labor; change production techniques; relocate overseas; and eliminate certain jobs altogether.

The substitution of automatic dishwashers for hand washing, and automatic tomato-picking machines for manual pickers, are examples of the substitution of machines for labor in response to higher wages. The switch from sales ladies behind each counter in five-and-dime stores to checkout lines, from waiter-served to self-service and fast-food restaurants, from full-service to self-service gasoline stations are among the responses to higher labor costs. So, too, are the absence of movie theater ushers and the wide use by restaurants of plastic utensils and paper plates, because they do not require dishwashing.

Minimum Wage and Racial Discrimination

The idea that it is sometimes necessary for some individuals to lower their price in order to sell their services offends the sensibilities of many people who support the minimum wage law as a matter of a moral conviction motivated by concern for equity in the distribution of income. However, white racist unions in South Africa, with different motivation, have also been supporters of minimum wage laws and equal-pay-for-equal-work laws for blacks.

> During South Africa's apartheid era, white workers supported wage regulation. White unionists "argued that in absence of statutory minimum wages, employers found it profitable to supplant highly trained (and usually highly paid) Europeans by less efficient but cheaper non-whites."[58]

Said the South African Economic and Wage Commission of 1925, supporting the Wage Act of the same year:

> While definite exclusion of the Natives from the more remunerative fields of employment by law has not been urged upon us, the same result would follow a certain use of the powers of the Wage Board under the Wage Act of 1925, or of other wage-fixing legislation. *The method would be to fix a minimum rate for an occupation or craft so high that no Native would be likely to be employed.* Even the exceptional Native whose efficiency would justify his employment at the high rate, would be excluded by the pressure of public opinion, which makes it difficult to retain a Native in an employment mainly reserved for Europeans.[59]

The New York Times reported in 1972 that in South Africa:

> Right wing white unions in the building trades have complained to the South African government that laws reserving skilled jobs for whites have broken and should be abandoned in favor of equal-pay-for-equal-work laws. . . . The conservative building trades made it clear that they were not motivated by concern for black workers but had come to feel that legal job reservation had been so eroded by government exemptions that it no longer protected the white worker.[60]

To understand how South Africa's job-reservation laws became eroded requires only two bits of information: during the post-World War II period, there was a significant building boom in the country; and black construction workers were willing to accept wages 80 percent lower than those paid to whites. Such a differential made racial discrimination in hiring a costly proposition—and made contravening job-reservation laws economically attractive. Firms that chose to hire whites instead of blacks paid dearly—$1.91 per hour versus $0.39 per hour. White racist unions recognized that equal-pay-for-equal-work laws (a variation of minimum wage laws) would lower the cost of racial discrimination and thus improve their competitive position in the labor market.

Laws requiring equal pay for equal work produce effects similar to those mandating payment of a minimum wage. In fact, "equal pay for equal work" became the rallying slogan of South Africa's white labor movement.

Keir Hardie, a British labor leader, was greeted with rotten eggs during his visit there in 1907, because he advocated equality between whites and Indians. "He was afterwards allowed to speak, however, when the workers found that he believed in 'equal pay for equal work' regardless of colour or creed."[61]

Declared the secretary of the apartheid era and avowedly racist Building Worker's Union: "There is no job reservation left in the building industry, and in the circumstances I support the rate for the job as the second-best way of protecting our white artisans."[62] A year later he stated that he would be prepared to allow black artisans into the industry provided that minimum wages were raised from Rand 1,40 to at least Rand 2,00 per hour and if the rate-for-the-job was strictly enforced.[63]

When Frederick Creswell became the country's minister of labor, he introduced the Wage Bill of 1925, saying: "If our civilization is going to subsist we look upon it as necessary that our industries should be guided so that they afford any men desiring to live according to the European standards greater opportunities of doing so, and we must set our face against the encouragement of employment merely because it is cheap and the wage unit is low."[64] In the 1930s, white workers approved of the wage board's efforts to extend statutory minimum wages to nonwhites. The Labour Party minister for posts and telegraphs complained that whites were being ousted from jobs by "unfair competition," particularly by the Indians in Natal. He urged that employers be forced to pay them the same wages they were paying whites.[65]

Intentions versus Effects

South Africa's racist unions, during its apartheid era, supported minimum wages and equal-pay-for-equal-work laws (rate-for-the-job) for blacks. Were the intentions the same among Americans who support minimum wage laws? A racial effect of those laws can be found in the absence of racial preferences on behalf of employers. The minimum wage law gives firms economic incentives to seek to hire only the most productive employees, meaning that the firms are less willing to hire and/or train less productive employees, a group that includes teenagers, particularly minority teenagers. But ignoring productivity differences between black and white workers, the laws provide an incentive to discriminate racially in hiring.

The reason is that the minimum wage law lowers the private cost of discriminating against the racially less-preferred person.

The fact that a well-intentioned policy such as the minimum wage law can foster and promote racial discrimination might be incomprehensible to some people. Therefore, it is useful to develop a nonracial example to illustrate the effects of such "price-setting."

Consider filet mignon and chuck steak. Assume—realistically—that consumers prefer the former. Then the question becomes: why is it, despite consumer preferences, that chuck steak sells at all? The fact is that chuck steak outsells filet mignon. How does something less preferred compete with something more preferred? It does so by offering what economists call "compensating differences." In other words, as you wheel your shopping cart down the aisle, chuck steak "says" to you, "I don't look as nice as filet mignon, I'm not as tender and tasty, but I'm not as expensive either. I sell for $4.00 a pound while filet mignon sells for $9.00." Chuck steak therefore in effect offers to "pay" you $5.00 per pound for its "inferiority," a compensating difference.

Suppose sellers of filet mignon wanted to raise their sales by colluding against the less-preferred competitor. What would be their most effective strategy? Short of getting a law passed prohibiting sales of chuck steak, it would be to push for a law establishing minimum prices for steak. What would be the effect of a minimum steak law of, say, $9 per pound for all steaks?

Put yourself in the position of the shopper wheeling his cart down the aisle after the enactment of such a law. Chuck steak now says to you, "I don't look as nice as filet mignon, I'm not as tender and tasty, and I sell for the same price as my preferred competitor, filet mignon. Buy me." That plea would fall on deaf ears. You would say to yourself, "Why should I buy chuck steak when it sells for the same price as filet mignon, which I prefer anyway?" Such a sentiment exemplifies the basic law of demand: the lower the cost of doing something, the more of it will be done. In this case, the cost of discriminating against, not selecting, chuck steak is effectively zero. Prior to the legislated minimum price, the cost of discriminating against chuck steak was $5.00 per pound, the difference in price.

The steak example applies to any mandated minimum price. In the case of minimum wage laws, a mandated minimum lowers the cost of—hence encourages—the indulgence of racial preference in the labor market.

Some might object to the validity of my example by saying that people are not the same thing as cuts of meat. That is true — just as steel balls are not the same as people. However, although steel balls and people are different, both obey the law of gravity. The independent influence of gravity on a steel ball's acceleration is 32 feet per second per second and its influence on a person is exactly the same. Similarly, quantities demanded for cuts of meat are influenced by the law of demand, and so are quantities demanded of a person's labor services.

To understand how the minimum wage can raise the probability of employer "preference indulgence" and racial discrimination, we must simply recognize that money income is not the only form of compensation businessmen earn.[66] Their compensation consists of *non*-money income as well. An employer prefers what he considers to be desirable, or more desirable, working conditions. They might include finer furniture, plusher carpets, prettier secretaries, and more likable employees. The quantity of these more desirable working conditions actually chosen depends on their costs in terms of foregone profits.

Suppose that an employer has a preference for white employees over black employees. And for expository simplicity, assume that the employees among whom he can choose are identical in terms of their productivity. If there is a statute like the minimum wage law, requiring that employers pay the same wage no matter who is hired, what are his incentives?[67] He must pay the black $7.25 per hour and the white $7.25 per hour. He must find some basis for choice. As a result of the minimum wage law, his choice cannot be based on economic criteria like differences in wages. It must be based on noneconomic criteria.

Obviously, race is a noneconomic criterion. If the employer has a preference for white workers, he can indulge it at zero cost. However, if there were no minimum wage and a black worker was willing to work for a lower wage, say $4 per hour, there would be positive costs to employer preference indulgence. In this example, it would be $3.25 per hour, the difference in wages per employee.

That's only one part of the story. The market would penalize the employer who chooses employees and pays them higher wages based on market-irrelevant criteria.[68] Some employers would hire blacks at the lower wage — in our example, $4 per hour. Doing so and thereby incurring lower production costs, these firms would reap above-normal profits. The firms would be able to underprice the racially discriminating firms, capturing a greater share of the market and attracting more investors. In addition, new competitors might enter the market, enticed by the above-normal profits. In their attempt to secure the cheaper black labor, they would bid up wages. The pressure would be toward wage equality between blacks and whites, or at least lower unemployment among blacks.[69] This line of reasoning gains additional weight when we consider that blacks experienced less unemployment at times of far greater racial discrimination.

American Union Support for Minimum Wage Laws

As is the case in South Africa and elsewhere, unions in the United States are also the major supporters of the minimum wage law. While our unions state different bases for that support, one must always remember that the *effects* of a policy are by no means necessarily determined by its *intentions*. But a good case can be made that the effects of the minimum wage law *are* its intentions. This can be readily understood if we consider, as economists do, that in some productive activities, low-skilled workers are substitutes for higher-skilled workers. And if the latter, through the use of government's coercive powers, can reduce or eliminate the employment of low-skilled workers, they can achieve monopoly power and command higher wages. A simple numerical example captures the essence of this strategy:

> Suppose a hundred yards of fencing can be produced by using either one highly skilled or three low-skilled workers. If the wage of an individual highly skilled worker is $100 per day, and that of his low-skilled counterpart is $35 per day, the firm would employ the high-skilled worker because labor costs ($100 versus $105) would be lower and profits higher.

The highly skilled worker might recognize that one of the ways to increase his bargaining power would be to advocate a minimum wage of, say, $50 per day in the fencing industry. The arguments that the highly skilled worker would use to gain political support would be those given by our politicians and union leaders: "to raise the standard of living," "prevent worker exploitation," "provide a living wage," "insure worker equality," and so forth. After the enactment of a $50-a-day minimum wage law, the high-skilled worker can now demand any wage up to $150 per day (what it would now cost to hire three low-skilled workers) and retain employment.[70] Prior to the enactment of the minimum wage of $50 per day, a highly skilled worker's demand for $150 per day would have cost him his job. The effect of the minimum wage is to price that worker's competition out of the market.

Whether the example given above accurately portrays the motives behind labor unions' support and their large lobbying expenditures in behalf of minimum wage increases is not really at issue. The effects of actions do not depend on intentions. Whatever the intentions, the effect is to price their competition out of the market.

The restrictive activities promoted by unions do reduce employment opportunities and the income of those priced out of the market. This suggests that union strategies to raise their members' wages must be accompanied by lobbying for government welfare programs. Why? Because if unemployment meant starvation, there might be considerable political resistance to higher mandated wages. Unions therefore have incentives to support subsidy programs for those denied access to jobs.[71] Thus, it is probable that unions will lead the support for income-subsidy programs, such as the Job Corps, the Comprehensive Training and Education Act, summer work programs, food stamps, public service employment, and welfare.

The resulting redistribution of income constitutes a subsidy from society at large—that is, from those who pay taxes to those who have used the powers of government to restrict or eliminate job opportunity. Income-subsidy programs disguise the true effects of labor market restrictions created by unions and other economic agents by casting a few crumbs to those denied jobs in order to keep them quiet, thereby contributing to the creation of a permanent welfare class.

U.S. Business Support for Minimum Wage Laws

Businessmen have also used the minimum wage law as a means to protect themselves from competition. When John F. Kennedy was a senator, he supported increases in the law as a way of protecting New England industry from competitors in the South.[72] Farmers have supported agricultural versions of the law in order to reduce competition. This particularly insightful comment was made by New York Representative Joseph Y. Resnick in 1966 on behalf of his constituents:

Mr. Chairman, I would like to point out to all the members of the Northeast and from the city what this legislation means to them. For one thing, Mr. Chairman, it means that the farmers of the Northeast can compete fairly with farmers from the rest of the country.

Now, Mr. Chairman, we have poultry farmers in our part of the country. Our farmers pay anywhere from $1.25 to $1.75 an hour for help. I ask you how can they compete with poultry farmers in Mississippi who pay $3 a day for a ten-hour day.[73]

There are other instances of business interests that are served by minimum wage requirements in U.S. territories and Puerto Rico—and more recently in Mexico, under the North American Free Trade Agreement. In those cases, the businessman's underlying desire is to reduce competition from lower-wage areas. Historically, for example, the minimum wage law got very little political support from low-wage states, especially those in the South.

Labor Market Myths

Before concluding our discussion of minimum wage laws, we should comment on several widely accepted labor market myths.

1. *If teenagers are allowed to work at subminimum wages, they will be employed while their parents go unemployed.* The statement assumes that there is a finite number of jobs available, i.e., that the acquisition of a job by one person necessarily means the loss of a job by another. There is no evidence to support the notion of a finite job total. The number of people employed by civilian enterprises in the United States grew from less than a million during colonial times to today's 151 million. As long as human wants remain limitless, so will the number of potential jobs. If youths were exempted from the provisions of minimum wage, there would be some substitution in employment, but the overwhelming effect would be that of increasing total employment.

2. *The employment problem faced by youths and others is that there are simply no jobs available.* If this myth is accepted at face value, it is the same as saying that all human wants have been satisfied. It asserts that no one anywhere wishes to have more of some goods or services that would create

employment opportunities for young people. There is no evidence to support such an assertion. As with other things of value, the quantity of labor hired conforms to the law of demand: the higher its price, the less it is used, and conversely. What people mean when they say no jobs are available is that none are at a "desirable" or mandated wage rate. Nothing is strange about this observation, because at some wage level anyone will find himself unemployable. For example, if the writer informed his employer that the minimum salary he would accept was $500,000 per year, there would simply be no job available for him at George Mason University. The difference between workers is that the wage that would cause some people to be unemployed is higher than that which would cause other people to be unemployed.

3. *Many people are unemployed because they have few skills and other qualifications.* Low skills can explain low wages but not unemployment. The history of blacks provides concrete evidence. A person is qualified or unqualified only in a relative sense—that is, relative to some wage. To speak of qualifications or skills in an absolute sense has little meaning. For example, a carpenter who is qualified, and hence employable, at a wage of $20 per hour, may be unqualified, and hence *un*employable, at $35 per hour. This principle applies to everything. A Sears suit is "unqualified" to sell for the same price as a hand-tailored Pierre Cardin suit.

Consider this interesting aspect of skills and qualifications: if an organization of, say, carpenters can through legal institutions mandate that employers pay all carpenters hired a wage of $35 per hour, then they have artificially disqualified and made unemployable the carpenter who used to find work paying $20 per hour.

This kind of artificial disqualification applies directly to the problems minorities face in the labor market. It is frequently said that they have a high unemployment rate because of their low skills. In earlier times, however, minorities had much *lower* unemployment rates. No one would or could explain that in terms of blacks during those periods having more education and training than they now do. The real reason is that through the political mechanism (intentionally and unintentionally), many blacks have been made artificially unqualified.

4. *Widespread automation causes high unemployment rates among a large sector of the labor force.* First, increases in relative wages are a proximate cause

of automation: when wages rise relative to capital costs, firms have incentives to substitute capital for labor. For example, when elevator operators successfully negotiated a higher wage, their success was followed, a few years later, by widespread installation of automatic elevators. After farm workers were brought under the minimum wage, we saw greater farm mechanization. Second, the automation-causes- unemployment argument assumes a finite number of jobs. The argument's implication is that society has no use for the labor saved by machinery. The very reason nations raise their higher standards of living is a result of capital being used to replace labor, thereby freeing up that labor to undertake other tasks. For example, in 1800, it took 95 out of every 100 Americans to feed the nation. Today, it takes less than three. Workers no longer needed to farm became available to produce thousands of other goods—and did produce them, as the breadth of the U.S. economy expanded tremendously.

5. *Higher minimum wages give workers increased purchasing power that in turn sustains high employment.* This myth assumes that workers keep their jobs and work the same number of hours as before. Some workers will and some will not. Those who lose their jobs as a result of a hypothetical right to earn $5.85 an hour will find that the hypothetical right will not buy groceries and housing. Furthermore, higher wages are not the same thing as more purchasing power when the artificial wage increases give rise to political forces to create inflation.

6. *The minimum wage law is an antipoverty weapon.* If this were true, we would have an instant solution to the world's poverty and underdevelopment problems. We would just advise countries to raise their minimum wage. The sad fact of life is that low-skilled workers are not so much underpaid as they are under-skilled. The way to help them is to make them more productive. This cannot be done with a stroke of the legislative pen.

7. *The poor benefit most from minimum wage increases.* The hard truths about the types of workers most likely to be employed at the minimum wage raise questions about the efficacy of the minimum wage law as an antipoverty tool. Eighty percent of all minimum wage workers live in non-poor households,[74] with almost 20 percent in households earning annual incomes above $50,000.[75] More than 50 percent of minimum wage earners are between sixteen and twenty-four years old, and more than 63 percent

work part-time. Only 5 percent of all working adults are paid the minimum wage.[76]

These labor market myths have maintained their popularity down through the ages, primarily because they have served particular interest groups and because many other people are decent and concerned about the welfare of their fellow man—but without understanding economics. But truly compassionate policy requires dispassionate analysis, and the debunking of these and other labor market myths is an important means to that end.

The minimum wage law has imposed incalculable harm on the most disadvantaged members of our society. The absence of work opportunities for many youngsters does not only mean an absence of pocket money. Early work opportunities provide much more than that: important insights on how to find a job and to adopt proper attitudes toward both, punctuality, and respect for supervision in the workplace. Lessons of that sort learned on any job help make a young person a more valuable and successful worker in the future. In addition, early work experiences give youngsters the pride and self-respect that come from being financially semi-independent. That is even more important for black youngsters, a disproportionate number of whom grow up in female-headed households and go to the nation's worst schools. If they are to learn job-related lessons, many of them will be learned *through* a job.

The Minimum Wage Vision

We observe people who share identical goals advocating different public policies, and quite often the policies produce unintended consequences. Many who profess concern for the welfare of low-skilled workers advocate higher minimum wage laws. Others, citing an identical concern, oppose higher minimum wage laws. One question we might ask is, how can honest and intelligent people, without a self-serving purpose, arrive at polar-opposite policy conclusions? The answer is that conclusions often depend on one's vision of how the world operates. For example, if one's initial premise, stated or not, is that an employer must hire a certain number of workers to do a particular job, the logic behind increasing the minimum wage law as a means to raise incomes of low-skilled workers is impeccable.

According to that vision, the minimum wage's only effects are higher wages for workers and lower profits for employers. [77]

That is a particularly optimistic vision of minimum wage laws. A higher minimum wage implies higher costs, but higher costs affect employment per se as well as wages and profits. They also affect the attitude of the firm's investors, who worry about return on equity. And if product prices are increased, the attitudes of both investors and customers may well turn negative. In other words, the vision falsely assumes that customers will not seek cheaper substitutes and will purchase the same quantities after the price increase as before, resulting in no negative impact on employment.

By contrast, other people start with the premise that employers are responsive to changes in the price of labor, stockholders are responsive to changes in equity value, and customers are responsive to product prices. These people may have just as much concern for the welfare of the low-skilled but nonetheless argue against increases in the minimum wage law. They see that employer responses to higher wages include: substitution of capital for labor (automation); employment of self-service techniques; relocation in a part of the country or the world that offers lower labor costs; and other measures that economize on the use of labor. Holders of this vision argue that mandated wage increases that exceed worker productivity will discriminate against the employment—and the on-the-job training—opportunities available to the lowest-skilled worker.

The view that ignores or perceives no response to changes in wages is what economists call zero elasticity of response. The vision it involves perceives that changes in the independent variable (wages) have no effect on the dependent variable (the amount of labor hired). This vision, in the public policy arena, has produced disastrous consequences.

Invisible Victims

Much of the political support for higher minimum wages reflects self-interest. It is, as we have discussed, a way for some workers to reduce competition with low-wage earners. Many others support minimum wage legislation because of an honest concern for the disadvantaged worker. They see people working under poorly paid, "sweatshop" conditions. They may see old women or illegal aliens working ten hours a day for $2 or $3 an hour. Having made these observations, they may summon the Department of Labor or report the employer to the Immigration and Naturalization Service. The factory owner may be fined for violations of wage-and-hour and immigration laws.

Having brought this action, do-gooders walk away triumphantly, thinking that justice has won over evil. Six months later, if they return to the factory, the people they see working are better off. They are earning the minimum wage and have better working conditions. This gives affirmation to the activists' sense of accomplishment.

What the do-gooders don't see are the people—the illegal aliens, the old women, the teenagers—who no longer have a job. The illegal may be back in Mexico, living under worse conditions. The old woman may be no longer earning any wage, and the kid may be on a street corner committing a crime. These are the invisible victims of the advocates' actions. Neither the victims nor their advocates make a connection between their worsened condition and increases in the minimum wage. Victims do not know why they cannot find a job, and are likely to chalk it up to "bad times" or racial discrimination rather than higher minimum wages.

Before the do-gooders "helped," they forgot to ask, why would anyone work ten hours per day for the paltry sum of $2 or $3 an hour? Would they have selected such a job if they had superior alternatives? The only conclusion is that the low-paying sweatshop job might be their best alternative. Such a person is indeed unfortunate, but they are by no means made better off by the destruction of that low-paying job.

The real problem is that workers are not so much underpaid as they are under-skilled. And the real task is to help those people *become* skilled. Congress cannot do this simply by declaring that as of such-and-such a date, everybody's productive output is now worth $7.25 per hour. This makes about as much sense, and does just about as much harm, as doctors "curing" patients simply by declaring that they are cured.

CHAPTER 4

Occupational and Business Licensing

People of the same trade seldom meet together, even for
merriment and diversion, but the conversation ends in a
conspiracy against the public, or in some other contrivance
to raise prices.
—Adam Smith, *Wealth of Nations*

FOR MANY BUSINESSES AND OCCUPATIONS, federal, state, and local governments regulate the conditions by which individuals may enter and conduct themselves.[1] The most often-stated justifications are to protect public health, safety, and morals, provide for orderly markets and a fair rate of return, and eliminate unscrupulous practitioners. Those are the stated, "public spirited" *intentions* of such regulation. Quite apart from them are its *effects*, which can be analyzed through economic analysis. To analyze the situation, we do not have to deny or even acknowledge the intentions. Stated intentions are one aspect of economic legislation; its effects are very different. The former often bear no relation to and may conceal policy results.

Control by government over the entry into an occupation is typically done through licensure laws. Some 800 occupations are licensed in at least one state.[2] They include such "learned" professions as medicine and law, plus others requiring considerably less training time—for example, barbers, cosmetologists, and plumbers. In many parts of the country, the occupations licensed include surprising choices: beekeepers, lightning rod installers, taxidermists, septic tank cleaners, tree surgeons, fortune tellers.[3]

People who practice a licensed trade without a license can be subjected to criminal prosecution and fines or imprisonment. Licensure laws have a variety of legal minimum requirements that must be satisfactorily met as a condition of entry. They can include: minimum schooling; citizenship; written, oral, or practical competency testing; attendance at government-approved schools or apprenticeship programs; prior occupational experience; and minimum age requirements.

There are also highly questionable licensing requirements, such as those California imposes on a would-be barber. In order to become a licensed barber, one must pass an examination that tests one's knowledge of the chemical composition of bones and the name of the muscle in the hyoid bone. Most states require barbers to receive instruction in bacteriology, histology of the hair, skin, nails, and nerves as well as instruction on diseases of the skin, hair, glands, and nails. The state of Georgia used to require those who seek to be a commercial photographer to pass a Wassermann test for syphilis. Some states authorize its cities and towns to make local residency a requirement for licensing plumbers, engineers, and other professions.[4]

The laws involved are usually administered by people who are selected from, or elected to, a board of commissioners by those who are already practicing the occupation or trade. These commissioners change and modify licensure requirements. They have state police powers at their disposal to enforce concurrence and compliance among practitioners.[5] About three-fourths of all licensing boards are composed solely of people working in the occupations that the boards control.[6]

The most immediate effect of licensing is to restrict the number of practitioners because of the higher entry costs involved in meeting the qualifications of the activity. Some licenses, as in the cases of cosmeticians and barbers, require many months of schooling. Others require the installation of costly health and safety equipment. Still others demand the purchase of the license or "certificate of authorization" from an incumbent practitioner that can cost millions of dollars, as was the case when interstate trucking was highly regulated. Further, some jurisdictions issue only a fixed number of licenses or authorizations. All of these requirements raise the cost of entry, which naturally leads to a smaller number of practitioners.

Restricting that number is only the initial effect of licensing. A secondary effect is that the price of the good or service offered is higher than it would otherwise be. The result of restricting entry to a business or occupation, and probably the primary intent of licensing, is to raise the incomes of incumbent practitioners. Evidence supports this self-interested behavior: (1) most licensure laws are the result of intense lobbying by incumbents, *not* of consumers demanding more protection from incompetent or unscrupulous practitioners; (2) when incumbents in an unlicensed trade lobby for licensing (or when those in one already licensed lobby for higher entry requirements) they virtually always seek a "grandfather" clause that exempts them from meeting the new requirements, leaving the burden of the higher entry costs to be borne mainly by new entrants; (3) practitioner violations of the licensing codes, such as price-cutting and extra hours, are nearly always reported to the licensing board by the incumbents rather than by customers.[7]

The severest form of occupational licensing is the kind that imposes a *fixed* number of licensed practitioners in addition to education, age, citizenship, and apprenticeship requirements. Numerical limits tend to produce the highest economic rewards for those already in the trade.[8] Legal restrictions on the number of practitioners in *occupations* are generally not set by statute. The right to set and modify the number of practitioners is done by unions, trade associations, and examining boards. Unions accomplish that through their power to set the number of apprenticeship or restricted union-membership openings and to use probationary status to adjust to transitory changes in demand for the services of their members.

Examining boards can control the rate of entry into an occupation by raising or lowering the pass rate of those taking the licensing examination. Often they will do this according to the earnings and employment conditions then current in the trade or profession.[9]

The reason why licensing statutes typically restrict entry by raising entry cost, and not by imposing limits on the number or practitioners, appears to be mostly political. Strategically, it is far more politically plausible, and publicly acceptable, for practitioners of a trade to justify higher entry requirements on the grounds that they raise standards and protect consumers against quacks than to base restrictions on the number of practitioners. Numerical restrictions must be argued on the ground of adverse third-party effects, such as that too many taverns will lead to drunkenness or too many taxis to traffic congestion. The liquor and taxicab industries, incidentally, exemplify business licensing in which many municipalities do impose numerical restrictions on practitioners.

In the practice of some trades, such as taxi driving and the sale of liquor, state permission to practice the trade is transferable. When licenses are sold on the market, it is possible to calculate the value to practitioners to do business under a state monopoly. The license price represents the present value of monopolistic income over the life of the business.

Taxicab Licensure

Perhaps the most egregious form of licensure involves New York City taxicabs. The municipal government requires a medallion for each operating cab.[10] The code also provides for regulation of taxi fares and other conditions of operation. The medallion system stemmed from the Haas Act of 1937. Under the act, the city sold medallions for $10 to all persons *then* operating taxis. Of the 13,566 original medallions issued, 1,794 were returned to the city during World War II by owners who went into the armed forces. Since 1937, no new medallions have been issued, except a recent 54 awarded for the operation of wheelchair-accessible vehicles. However, some of the medallions turned in have been *re*issued, raising the total to 12,241. The number of medallions sets the upper limit on the number of taxis that may operate within the city. The owner of a medallion pays a small annual fee, but the medallion itself and the rights it confers on the owner constitute valuable private property. As such, the transferable medallion commands a market price, and that price has risen inexorably and sharply:

> In 1937, as stated, one could buy an original for $10. In 1947, the medallion price rose to $2,500. By 1960, it was $28,000; 1970, $60,000; 1998, $200,000; and in May 2007, a taxi medallion sold for $600,000.[11] In May 2010, individual medallions sold for $603,000 and a corporate medallion for $781,000.[12] In practice, the initial outlay is less because some New York banks will lend up to 80 percent of the medallion price.[13] In addition, there are firms, such as Medallion Financial Corporation, that specialize in underwriting these purchases. In 2007, Medallion Financial

Corporation had $520,000,000 outstanding in taxi-medallion loans.[14] Taxi-medallion prices can be readily explained. If the taxi industry were run on free-market principles, open to all potential sellers, the market value of a medallion would be zero. But with government-controlled entry, which confers monopoly power on incumbent taxi owners, and with medallions transferable, they command a price. The present value (selling price) of the medallion represents, and is a measure of, the value of the higher earnings taxi owners enjoy as a result of being able to sell taxi services in a government-protected, monopoly market.

In other words, the value of the medallion shows what the buyer is willing to pay for government protection from free-market competition.[15] How much above-normal profit would justify a medallion bidder paying $500,000 in order to do business in a monopolized market? One way to estimate that is to ask how much $500,000 would yield sitting in a bank and earning a 6 percent interest rate. At 6 percent, the yield would be $30,000 per annum. Thus, it is safe to assume that bidders expect monopoly profits worth at least that much.

New York's medallion system keeps the supply of taxis restricted. The inevitable result is that when public demand for taxi services increases, the response is mostly in the form of higher fares and possibly poorer-quality service. This is the natural result of monopolized markets: the tendency of higher prices and lower-quality service when a seller is insulated from open-market competition. Another way of looking at the total value of medallions is that it is a measure of the transfer of income from taxi riders to medallion owners—who often do not drive their own cabs but lease their medallion to people who do.

The Entrepreneurial Response to the Taxi Monopoly

Several communities have responded to the medallioned-taxicab monopoly and inferior transportation services. In New York, this response has in part taken the form of illegal or "gypsy" cabs. The emergence of gypsies is substantially a direct response to the failure of the medallioned industry to provide an adequate level of taxi services. Neighborhoods such as Harlem, Bedford-Stuyvesant, Brownsville, and the South Bronx, to name a few, have consistently received poor taxi service from the medallioned industry. Many residents in these communities simply installed meters, painted signs and put lights on their private cars, declared them taxis, and cruised the neighborhoods, providing transportation for hire. An estimated 30,000 gypsy taxis operate in New York City.[16] These are people earning an honest, albeit illegal, living providing needed services.

High risks of robberies and other violence are some of the reasons the medallioned-taxi industry give for not providing services in these communities. In addition, the operators perceive these areas as being economically unprofitable compared to the central business district and other parts of the city. (Some taxi drivers require customers to pay in advance if they are being taken to "rougher" neighborhoods.) To a significant degree, these perceptions are correct. Richard Marosi writes, "Driving a gypsy cab is one of the most dangerous jobs in New York City. Since 1990, 180 drivers—an average of over two a month—have been killed while on duty, according to the New York City Taxi and Limousine Commission."[17]

Such a large illegal operation is possible for two reasons: (1) poor services by the medallioned industry; (2) failure of the authorities to rigorously enforce the law against gypsy drivers as long as their operations are limited to New York's poor, high-crime neighborhoods. The Taxi and Limousine Commission, the courts, and recent mayors have shown a reluctance to suppress illegal taxi operations—in no small part because of the poor services provided by the medallioned industry. However, when gypsy drivers, emboldened by their successes at ignoring the law, operate in the more lucrative central business district, other higher-income areas, and at the airports, they encounter greater resistance.

New York's gypsy-taxi industry is a combination of illegal and semi-legal operators. The semi-legal component consists of private "livery" drivers. Private liveries are not licensed by the City of New York. They may operate a vehicle for hire if they are licensed by the *State* of New York as an "omnibus." But livery drivers are required by law to obtain *all* of their business by telephone or off-the-street requests; they are not allowed to cruise for fares. This distinction between private liveries and taxicabs has broken down in recent years. A study done for the Taxi Policy Institute reports, "[W]e estimate that over 100,000 liveries a day illegally attempt to pick up passengers just in Midtown."[18] An earlier study reported that "at least 75 percent of private livery business is obtained by passenger hails while cruising along the street. That is, private liveries conduct their business in a fashion reserved by law for medallioned taxis."[19]

Because of prohibitions by the New York State Human Rights Commission, no reliable figures exist on the racial composition of taxi owners and private livery drivers (and much less about gypsy taxis). But according to one early estimate, nearly 95 percent of all livery drivers were either black or Puerto Rican.[20]

The flourishing gypsy operation in New York is indicative of at least several important factors. Above-normal profits are currently being earned in New York's legal taxi industry. Simple economic theory predicts that when that happens, outsiders look to get in and share the wealth. The fact that many of the operators in the illegal part of the taxi business are black, Puerto Rican, and/or members of other minority groups shows that it is relatively easy to provide a socially valuable service. Evidence is twofold: patrons are willing to pay; and the service has existed for more than four decades. The fact of a robust gypsy-taxi operation proves that these producers are capable of adapting to the environment and can fill a need not being filled by the medallioned industry.

Although the medallioned operators allege that they cannot provide services to the ghetto because of high crime and unprofitability, gypsy cabs manage to do just that. Most important, the flourishing gypsy-cab business has significant implications for other areas of economic life. As noted above, members of New York's black, Puerto Rican, and other minority groups get a chance to earn an honest, although technically illegal, livelihood—providing taxi services by openly disregarding monopolistic laws. There are many other areas of economic life in which those people could compete on equal footing. But in those areas, the barriers to entry are institutionally and legally enforced.

Taxicab Operations in other Cities

Most major cities have restricted taxicab entry requirements. Some do so by means of costly prices for licenses: Chicago ($56,000), Boston ($285,000),[21] Philadelphia ($75,000); others require that the entrant obtain a certificate of "public convenience and necessity" (CPCN) that is typically issued by a public utility commission.

Typical of the latter is taxicab regulation in Denver. The Colorado Public Utilities Commission (PUC) and the state legislature regulate the taxicab industry there. In Denver, for example, one must obtain a CPCN that is issued by the PUC; an applicant must demonstrate that adequate taxi services are not being provided *and* that existing companies cannot provide them. Starting in 1946, and as late as 1995, every application to operate a new taxi company in the city of Denver was denied.

The Colorado PUC had no objective criteria that established just what qualifies as "substantial inadequacy" of service. If the applicant appeared to be nearing those criteria, attorneys for existing taxi companies merely showed up at the hearing and declared that their clients had the ability to provide the allegedly inadequate service and asserted that the applicant's entry would be a duplication.

As a result of impossible entry criteria, the Denver taxicab market consisted of three companies: Metro Taxi, Yellow Cab, and Zone Taxi. Each was started during the 1930s and "grandfathered in" when the existing legislation was passed. While these companies are rivals, they cooperate with one another—with the assistance of the Colorado PUC—to forestall entry by prospective new competitors.

In July 1992, Quick Pick Cabs, formed by four black taxi drivers, filed an application for a CPCN. The three Denver taxi companies, along with ten others operating elsewhere in Colorado, intervened to protest Quick Pick's application; indeed, three of the companies were represented by the same law firm. Taking advantage of PUC requirements, the lawyers served on the upstart black drivers nearly 100 interrogatories, seeking such information as:

> the entire expense and anticipated expense of Applicant's advertising and the anticipated revenues to be used for such advertising by the Applicant including the media used or to be used, the amount of times ads have been or will be placed in that media; any circulars and the distribution points of such circulars; who published or will publish the circulars for the Applicant and, the dates and amounts and/or values of any advertising contracts paid or to be paid for by the Applicant.[22]

Additional interrogatories included requests for names of prospective employees and other costly-to-produce documents designed to intimidate the new applicant. In November 1992, the PUC held a hearing and summarily denied Quick Pick's application for not having met the requirements for approval.

Some interesting features of Denver's existing taxi industry can be found in the affidavits of the plaintiffs.[23] Each plaintiff except Reverend Oscar S. Tillman was a taxicab driver who worked for Yellow Cab. They all owned their taxis. But according to PUC regulations, they had to operate under a license owned by Yellow Cab. In order to do that, they had to pay the company $600 to have each of their vehicles painted in taxicab colors and design, and also have a meter and radio installed. In addition, they had to give Yellow Cab what is known as a "payoff"—an upfront, weekly fee for the privilege of using the company's license.[24] Moreover, each owner-driver was responsible for gasoline, maintenance, and other related costs of operation.

The plaintiffs argued that the payoff system forced them to look for long-haul rides rather than provide services for senior citizens and poor people, who mostly use taxis for shorter and hence less profitable hauls. Thus, the poorer sections of Denver remained ill-served by taxis.

In 1993, the Washington, D.C.-based Institute for Justice filed a lawsuit on behalf of the four Denver taxicab applicants. *Leroy Jones et al. v. Colorado Public Utilities Commission* challenged the PUC-created taxicab monopoly and the regulatory procedures that perpetuate it as a violation of the equal protection clause of the Fourteenth Amendment. In August of that year, a district court dismissed the plaintiff's challenge to the Denver taxi monopoly. Their attorneys appealed to the U.S. Court of Appeals for the Tenth Circuit.

Their case was made moot by the Colorado legislature in 1995, when it modified the state's PUC taxicab regulation for large cities. The state's larger cities now have what is called regulated competition, which places a presumption in favor of new applicants and a burden on the PUC to show why applications should not be approved. As a result of the new legislation, two of the Institute for Justice clients, Leroy Jones and Ani Ebong, created Freedom Cabs, the first new taxi company in Denver since 1947. As an interesting aside, it was the local branch of the NAACP, not the national office, that assisted the institute in winning the right for Freedom Cabs to operate. The national office refused to give assistance.

Other Regulatory Reforms

Despite its growing population, Minneapolis has for decades limited its number of licensed taxis to 343, denying entry to would-be owner-operators. In March 2007, the city instituted reforms in its taxi ordinance. They authorized the semi-annual issuance of 45 new licenses through 2010; and by 2011, the government-imposed limit will be eliminated altogether. Under the new ordinance, a prospective entrant will have to meet the standard of being "fit, willing and able," as opposed to being obligated to meet the older standard of having to show "public convenience and necessity" for that service; that subjective test favored incumbent owners, who would show up at hearings to protest against the issuance of additional taxi licenses. The new ordinance would also permit license applicants to apply for a license without being required first to join one of the existing taxi companies, thus ending their gatekeeper power.

The Minneapolis Taxicab Owners Association sued the city, making self-serving claims. Among them: additional taxis would create more traffic congestion; there was no demand for more taxis; and opening the taxi market would jeopardize the value of licenses that could be sold for as much as $24,000. In *Minneapolis Taxi Owners Coalition, Inc. v. City of Minneapolis*, the judge ruled against the coalition, saying, "The [established] taxi vehicle license holders do not have a constitutionally protected freedom from competition." He recommended dismissal of the suit to overturn the free-market reforms, and a federal district court subsequently adopted that recommendation.

The Taxicab Industry in Washington, D.C.

The industry in the nation's capital differs markedly from that found in most other major metropolitan areas. For all intents and purposes, it offers *open* entry to outsiders. The local public-service commission controls fares and such other conditions of operation as vehicle safety and insurance requirements. By comparison, the price of a license is stunningly low: "The Chairperson shall collect a fee of five ($5.00) for each license issued."[25]

As of 1979, there were about 8,400 taxis operating in the District of Columbia. Approximately 90 percent of the taxis were owner-operated.

Nowadays, the largest fleet operator in the city is the Yellow Cab Company. Yellow Cab has forty vehicles. In addition, it franchises its name to about 900 independent owner-operators. But the company controls only its own forty.

Consumer groups and owner-operators have always fought against placing numerical limits on the number of taxis in the city. A typical statement expressing their attitude:

> Considering the monopolistic trend that all similar (referring to numerical limitations) practices have taken in other cities where they have been put into operation, it seems as though we could, here in Washington, profit by the mistakes of those who have preceded us in this taxi-control problem. This is the Capitol of the United States and the seat of the Federal Government and as such it is advisable that we shun any legislation that is monopolistic in nature for it is the duty of the Federal Government to oppose monopolies, not to foster them.[26]

Similar sentiments were expressed by the Taxicab Industry Group, a loosely knit owner-operator association that represents 43 of the 62 taxi companies and associations and 85 percent of the drivers operating in D.C.:

> The taxi business is unique here in that approximately 90 percent of the cabs are owner-operated. Therefore, passengers get a better and safer ride because of the driver's personal interest in his own taxicab. This is not true in other large cities where meters are required and the operation of the taxi system is controlled by fleets. Because he is an independent businessman, as we have previously stated many times, the owner-operator has better equipment and exercises greater care than a driver who is not an owner. It is the independent cab drivers in Washington, D.C., who have given the city the best taxi service of any city in the United States. This is a recognized fact, testified to by the many visitors who ride our cabs as well as many Senators and Congressmen who travel worldwide and know firsthand about good services.[27]

Washington taxi owners' strong stand against monopolization of their industry is not so much an expression of an ideological persuasion to free

markets as the fear that monopolization would benefit and foster companies with largess at the expense of the independent owner-operator.[28]

Thanks to open entry, the Washington taxi industry consists of mostly
self-employed people who work and conduct their business as they see
fit. It has been estimated that at least 50 percent of the taxi owners are
part-time operators who work after and before hours spent at other jobs.
In addition, a number of owners lease their taxis to family members and
other individuals on either a full-time or part-time basis.

The relatively free market that exists in Washington produces business
ownership or work opportunities for many semi-skilled workers, college
students, and others wishing to supplement their regular earnings. The
Washington experience also refutes the disorderly market, "dog-eat-dog,"
and congestion arguments used as justification for strict regulation in
other cities. Consumers benefit immensely. Washington had one taxi per
71 citizens, while New York has one taxi per 615.

A Foreign Experience with Taxi Deregulation

The interests and behavior of those who seek to close markets tend to
be the same in the United States and elsewhere. Political pressure from
incumbent taxi license holders caused the government of Ireland to limit
the number of licenses. Dublin numbered 1,800 of them in 1978. By 1997,
there were 1,974. Between 1980 and 2000, a dramatic increase in Ireland's
GDP brought a 63 percent increase in the number of persons employed;
*un*employment plummeted from 18.6 percent to 3.7 percent, and the
number of overseas visitors increased from 2 million to 6 million a year.
According to one estimate, had taxi numbers kept pace with real GDP,
there would have been at least 4,200 Dublin taxis—well over twice the
actual count in 1997.[29]

As in New York City, there was in Dublin a secondary market for taxi
licenses. As a result of entry restrictions, coupled with a higher demand
for taxi services, the city's taxi license prices increased from 3,500 Irish
pounds ($7,350) in 1980 to 90,000 Irish pounds ($103,000) by 2000.
Also, as in New York City and elsewhere, there was a separation between
people who held the licenses and taxi drivers who rented them. One report
estimated that the drivers who rented a license paid about 50 percent of
the revenue they earn to the license holder. They have therefore been lik-
ened to urban sharecroppers.[30]

In 2000, Ireland's taxi industry was deregulated. In 2000, there were 3,913 taxis in the entire country; by 2002, 11,630, a 297 percent increase. In Dublin in 2000, there were 2,722 taxis; by 2002, 8,609, a 316 percent increase. License prices fell from 90,000 Irish pounds to the government's set price of 7,000 Irish pounds. The large increase in the number of cabs after deregulation significantly reduced passenger waiting times and is expected to reduce the price of taxi rides.

A Taxi Hardship Panel was set up to address persistent complaints of financial suffering by taxi license holders following deregulation. Ireland's courts have said that the state has no legal duty to compensate license holders as a result of the collapse in license prices. Nonetheless, the panel has made several recommendations for a payment of 12.6 million Euros ($18 million).[31] One might speculate that the possibility of incumbent license holders receiving compensation might have made taxi deregulation in Ireland more politically feasible.

Jitney Services

A jitney is a small vehicle such as a car, minibus, or van that travels a fixed or semi-fixed route picking up passengers for small fares. "Jitney" was once the common term for a nickel—the amount typically charged passengers. The first jitneys appeared in Los Angeles in 1914. They flourished, and by 1915, more than 60,000 of them were operating in 175 cities. Their success was mainly due to passenger dissatisfaction with electric streetcars and the demonstrated fact that the jitney was a viable substitute during strikes by trolley men. By 1920, jitneys virtually disappeared because of the political clout held by the streetcar industry that responded to jitneys taking away much of their business. They used their clout to enact legislation that restricted or banned jitney operation.

During the 1920s, Houston, along with most municipal authorities, did away with jitneys. Whatever the stated purpose for those actions, their objective was to provide monopoly protection for competing industries— the streetcar and later the bus.

In 1989, the Center for Civil Rights of the Kansas City, Missouri-based Landmark Legal Foundation, brought suit to end Houston's prohibition of jitney services. The plaintiff, Alfred Santos, a former taxi driver, established a jitney service that operated in the mostly Hispanic section of east Houston, where the residents are poor and lack adequate transportation.

His service, joined by others, offered an efficient alternative to the city's monopolized, inefficient, costly bus service. Competition with the bus service brought retaliation, and the city, using threats of fines and imprisonment, shut down Santos' jitney operation. In 1994, U.S. District Judge John D. Rainey permanently enjoined the City of Houston from enforcing its ordinance banning jitney services, calling the ordinance arbitrary, outdated, and without a valid purpose.[32]

New York City Van Services

In 1997, the Institute for Justice filed a lawsuit in the State Supreme Court of New York on behalf of several minority entrepreneurs who operate commuter van services in New York City.[33] Those services first appeared in large numbers in the city in 1980, during a city-wide strike of public transportation workers. Industrious New Yorkers, primarily from New York's Caribbean communities, moved in to provide inexpensive van service. Their "dollar" vans operated along fixed routes, picking up and discharging passengers. After the strike ended, the vans continued to provide a service their customers saw as superior to the city's public transportation system.

Until 1993, the New York State Department of Transportation regulated the van service. Although the process for obtaining an operating license was tedious and expensive, the department regularly approved new van companies—but allowed them to provide only limited, pre-arranged service. Competition from even this limited service was entirely unacceptable to New York City's mass-transportation interests. In 1993, those forces used their political power to lobby the legislature to enact a law allowing the city to take over the task of regulating van transportation.

One need not speculate about the self-serving motives behind the strong industry support for a transportation law that empowered the city council to impose severe restrictions on the licensing of new van companies. Statements made in support of the law left no question. City-franchised bus companies and officials of the Transport Workers Union complained about the loss of revenue resulting from illegal vans operating in a "predatory " fashion on bus routes.

Patrick Condren, president of Metro Apple Express, a city-franchised bus company, complained, "We have a problem with illegal vans operating

in a predatory fashion in front of our routes . . . . we have a damn big problem when people are stealing people in front of us. . . . We have seen about
a million dollars a year moved over to the vans right in front of us. . . ."[34]
Damaso Seda, president of the Transport Workers Union, when asked
about his support for the bill, replied, "How about to protect our jobs,
would that meet your criteria, protecting civil service jobs?"[35] City Council
Member Archie Spigner argued that the self-employed van drivers should
not be permitted to displace unionized bus drivers who "make $15 an
hour, and . . . get vacations and holidays and every conceivable benefit,
and after 25 years on the job of driving a bus, then they receive a pension
for the rest of their lives."[36]

One council member summed up the anti-competitive motivation
behind the restrictions when he recalled working as a counsel to a state
senator:

> [I]t became readily apparent to me when I was meeting with the repre-
> sentatives from the Transport Workers Union, [and] the Transit authority
> and related agencies . . . that what they were really after was to pulverize
> and eviscerate and get rid of competition, a competitive force . . . this
> bill, if we indeed pass it, will be anti-immigrant, it will be anti-minority,
> it will be anti-competitive, . . . it undermines the very values that many
> of us stand for when we say that we . . . want to foster competition in our
> economy. What are we getting for that? We are going to get more public
> monopoly or quasi public monopoly of these private bus companies
> that . . . are just seeking some protection from competition.[37]

After 1993, the city routinely refused to authorize new commuter van
services. The 406 vans that have the required authorization operate under
restrictions that totally prohibit them from providing the service customers demand. Individuals who depend on van services want to be picked
up, as needed, at central locations (such as subway stops and shopping
centers) and driven home. The law also made it illegal for a van to pick up
customers unless they called in advance; and prohibited vans from operating along any bus route, driving them off virtually every major street in
the city.

City law now requires individuals who want to provide van services
to obtain three separate types of licenses. A would-be entrepreneur must

show that his van is insured and his drivers competent and trustworthy. The applicant must prove that additional service is required by the "present or future public convenience and necessity." This standard creates a presumption in favor of existing companies and places on an applicant the burden of assembling an unspecified amount of evidence to be evaluated by the Taxi and Limousine Commission. Finally, the law gives public bus companies undue influence over the outcome of the application process. Any bus company threatened with competition by the applicant has the right to object to the authorization. If that happens, and it always does, the applicant must show that the existing mass transit system is inadequate. The law fails to set forth any criteria or standards by which to measure the "adequacy" of mass transit.

Throughout the application process, city bureaucrats have unfettered discretion to deny an application for any reason, or for no reason at all. The city need not offer any guidance about what information an application should contain, nor is it required to explain why an application has been denied. In fact, the commission can deny one by simply doing nothing for 180 days after an application is submitted, even if the applicant proves that his service is necessary. Finally, even if the applicant secures the agency's approval, the city council retains the right to exercise a veto. Because public transportation interests exert an inordinate amount of influence over the council, it usually exercises this option. Those interests—the New York Metropolitan Transit Authority, private bus companies with city franchises, and the union representing public transportation workers—want competitors off the road.

In 1999, the New York State Supreme Court struck down as unconstitutional the law giving the New York City Council the power to reject van licenses already approved by the commission. Although further litigation is pending concerning the highly restrictive conditions under which licenses are issued and the conditions under which licensees must operate, this minor victory means that the council can no longer unilaterally overrule the commission's license decisions. The dollar vans still operate in the face of onerous regulations, and they serve thousands of passengers per day.

Racial Effects of Occupational and Business Licensing

Occupational licensing raises entry costs through various requirements: age, minimum secondary-school education, special schooling, citizenship, and license fees. Nobody is explicitly rejected; many decide not to try in the first place. The requirements are more problematic for some demographic groups than others. For example, the possession of a high school diploma will impose a greater burden on those groups with a higher high-school dropout rate.

Some licensing examinations consist of both written and "performance" parts. This introduces considerable bias, particularly when the written portion is of little significance in predicting the presence or absence of practical, performance talents. Applicants with better or more education obviously have greater facility with written expression. Others who have a limited reading ability, or whose native language is not English, suffer a disadvantage even if they perform well on the performance part.

Licensing requirements often specify a minimum number of hours of specialized education at "approved" schools. In addition, schooling requirements involve tuition and other costs, which exclude on the basis of available financial resources. That bias will of course not be evenly spread across all demographic groups.

Licensing of Cosmetologists

Cosmetology is the art or profession of applying cosmetics. Most practitioners perform operations that a woman might do herself at home, such as manicuring and hair washing and styling. Nonetheless, the practice of cosmetology for money is licensed in all states.

Stuart Dorsey studied the distributional effects of occupational licensing of cosmetologists in Missouri and Illinois.[38] He found that, in both states, the black failure rates were two to three times what would be expected if race and failure rate were unrelated. In the Missouri sample, only 3 percent of successful applicants were black, while they constituted 21 percent of failures. Similar results were obtained in the Illinois sample: black applicants accounted for 38 percent of failures but only 11 percent of successes. The Dorsey study further reported that black examination scores averaged more than ten points lower than whites when years of education and training were held constant.

Illinois and Missouri require that cosmetology applicants pass both a performance test and a written test in order to qualify for a license. The score on the former is based upon the quality of work done on a person chosen by the applicant as a model. At the time applicants take the performance test, they are unaware of their score on the written portion. Dorsey reports that the overall performance failure rate is very low—in Missouri, 13 percent; in Illinois, 5 percent. More remarkable is that the characteristics that were statistically significant in written examinations (race, education, and apprenticeship) have no explanatory value for the score on the practical exams. In other words, on the practical test, *race had no statistical significance* as an explanatory variable for pass rates.

It is therefore clear that the written examination acts to exclude applicants, mainly by race, who are just as productive as others according to so-called performance results. The Dorsey study concluded that the occupational licensing of cosmetologists: (1) screens out people on the basis of characteristics unrelated to job performance; and (2) causes an overinvestment in education and formal training—because much of the required training does not improve productivity, as measured by performance, and therefore is individually and socially wasteful. In addition, licensing serves to reinforce formal educational handicaps suffered by disadvantaged minorities who attend grossly inferior schools.

Empirical evidence bears out the theoretical expectations made by economists about the adverse racial effects of occupational licensure. Furthermore, the exclusion of disadvantaged people—who are qualified according to practical tests—does not support the public-interest arguments that are so often made for occupational licensing. Instead, the consuming public is worse off in having to put up with higher prices and longer queues. The only clear beneficiaries of occupational licensing are incumbent practitioners who can charge higher prices—and hence enjoy higher incomes—and answer to lower accountability standards as a result of their monopolized market.

The Case of Monique Landers

In 1993, Monique Landers was a 15-year-old Wichita high school student who had become a participant in the New York-based National Foundation for Teaching Entrepreneurship. Among NFTE's objectives is introducing minority youngsters to the world of entrepreneurship by teaching them to devise business plans and then helping them start an actual business. Businesses established by the program's youthful participants include: car washers and detailers; party magicians; stereo equipment installers; and babysitters. Monique's business plan won a $750 grant that she used to buy business cards, posters, and other business-related materials to start a hair-braiding business named A Touch of Class, where she braided the hair of friends and family for $15 to $20 per session.

A Touch of Class was so successful that Monique was invited to New York City by NFTE to be honored as one of its five Outstanding High School Entrepreneurs. That was when her trouble started. A local newspaper published the story about her award. Having read about Monique's success, several beauty-school operators and hundreds of angry hairdressers complained to the Kansas Cosmetology Board about Monique's lack of a license. In the name of public health and safety, the Kansas state board issued a formal warning to Monique, informing her that it was illegal for her to touch hair for a profit without a license. And if she did not immediately cease her practice, she would be subject to a fine and/or 90 days imprisonment in the county jail. Nancy Shobe, the board's director, suggested that, if Monique wished to become licensed, she should take a year-long cosmetology program at a certified school.

According to Frederic Laurino, owner of Vernon's Kansas School of Cosmetology, "This is a matter of morals. I feel sorry for the young lady. But I feel sorrier that a young lady in an entrepreneurship program at school has been taught to break the law."[39] Clint Bolick, litigation director for the Institute for Justice, remarked that the case is equivalent to restaurant boards shutting down kids' lemonade stands in the name of protecting public health and safety.

While the stated motivation for closing A Touch of Class is that of protecting public health and safety, the real purpose was to protect the monopoly power and incomes of established practitioners to braid hair per se. Braiding does not violate Kansas law; that happens only when money is involved, thereby threatening the incomes of incumbent cosmetologists. The larger irony of this case is that while the authorities cannot shut down youthful drug trafficking and crime in our metropolitan areas, they can successfully throttle youngsters engaging in an honest, though illegal, pursuit.[40]

The Cornwell Case

In 1997, the Institute for Justice filed a lawsuit—*Cornwell v. California Board of Barbering and Cosmetology*—in the federal district court in San Diego, challenging California's licensing practices as applied to practitioners of African hairstyling. The plaintiffs in this suit were Dr. JoAnne Cornwell and the American Hairbraiders & Natural Haircare Association, on behalf of its members. The action alleged violations of the Fourteenth Amendment's equal protection, due process, and privileges and immunities guarantees as well as similar guarantees under California's constitution. African hairstyling (e.g., braiding and corn-rowing, locking, twisting, and weaving) is a form of natural styling that does not use chemicals or other harsh processes that alter hair texture.

In the name of protecting public health, California requires that an individual who seeks to perform any kind of hairstyling service must complete nine months (1,600 hours) of classes at a state-approved cosmetology school, at a tuition cost of at least $5,000, before taking the state licensing examination. This regimen is required even though the school curriculum and the exam bear little or no relation to the kind of services rendered by African hairstylists.

The district court struck down California's cosmetology licensing scheme as it applies to those stylists. In rendering his decision, federal Judge Rudi Brewster said that requiring African hairstylists to comply with the state's cosmetology regulations "failed to pass constitutional muster" under the due process and equal protection clauses of the Fourteenth Amendment, adding that the training requirement in the case was "wholly irrelevant to the achievement of the state's objectives." Judge Brewster concluded that enough was enough, explaining "there are limits to what the State may require before its dictates are deemed arbitrary and irrational."

Other Adverse Effects of Licensing

Restricted entry through licensing places disadvantaged people at a severe handicap without necessarily improving the quality of services received by the consumer, the ostensible beneficiary of the regulation. In fact, one study showed that there is a significant relationship between occupational licensing and the number of accidental deaths by electrocution: the more stringent the state's electrician licensing examination, the fewer the electricians and higher prices for an electrician's services; therefore, the greater the willingness of amateurs to undertake electrical wiring tasks and risk electrocution in the process.[41]

Occupational licensing also produces what authors Sidney Carroll and Robert Gaston call the "Cadillac effect." By insisting on stiff requirements for entry, licensing provides high-quality services for high-income people. But people with *low* incomes, who cannot afford to pay the higher prices, are forced to do without the service, do the work themselves, or rely on low-priced, unlicensed charlatans.

There is evidence that occupational licensing is used in other ways that handicap minorities—for example, when incumbent practitioners attempt to protect their income in the face of a slack market for their services. Professor Alex Maurizi investigated the relationships between such a market in licensed occupations and the examination pass rate.[42] He found that the excess demand explained a substantial, and statistically significant, portion of the pass rate. When there was high unemployment in the licensed trade, the difficulty level of the exam rose in order to reduce the number of new entrants. Obviously, such a technique to protect the incomes of incumbents will have its greatest discriminatory impact on the groups in the population who have had a lower-quality education. Minorities are disproportionately represented in such a population.

This discussion would be incomplete without mentioning that blacks are not the only group targeted for discriminatory licensing. During the 1930s, virtually every occupational licensure law was amended to add U.S. citizenship as a new requirement. What public health and safety interest is served by the stipulation that an otherwise-qualified tradesman be a U.S. citizen? None. The 1930s saw an increasingly hostile racial climate in Europe, resulting in a large migration of Jews to the United States. Many of those immigrants, who included non-Jews as well, were skilled artisans. The U.S. citizenship requirement was an effective way to forestall their entry into licensed occupations, which served the interests of incumbent licensees.[43]

Conclusion

To criticize occupational licensing laws is not to argue that information about the quality of a licensee's services is not important to consumers. However, it is by no means clear that licensing is the most effective way to provide that information. Indeed, licensing may lower the "received" quality of the service in question. By making entry costs higher, there are fewer practitioners, which, as noted above, increases the cost of the service rendered and leads some consumers to resort to do-it-yourself methods that generally result in a lower-quality end product. For example, even the electrician who failed a licensing examination, scoring 65 when a score of 70 was necessary to pass, is likely to know more about electrical work and safety measures than the average consumer who undertakes a do-it-yourself project because he cannot afford to hire a licensed practitioner.

In addition, higher standards imposed by licensing requirements make consumers as a whole worse off. A spectrum of quality, from high to low, is consistent with the optimal stock of goods and services. Being forced to purchase a higher-quality good or service, when a lower quality would suffice or is what the customer wants, hurts consumers economically. For example, in the name of safety, a law could be enacted requiring that the only cars that can be sold are those whose occupants would emerge uninjured after a fifty-mile per hour collision. However, such cars would cost so much that most people could not afford to buy them. The existence of less crashworthy cars is clearly part of the optimal stock. People are always better off if they have knowledge about quality and the right to choose quality levels.

There are methods to produce information about quality without having the restrictions imposed by occupational licensing. Certification is one method. A practitioner can take a test and, if he scores in the 90s, have the right to declare himself a Class A practitioner; an 80, a class B practitioner; and so on. Such a method would give consumers information about quality while leaving them free to choose.

Professor Walter Gellhorn gives an insightful summation of the motives behind occupational licensing:

> Although ostensibly required to protect the public, licensing almost always impedes only those who desire to enter the occupation or "profession;" those already in practice remain entrenched without a demonstration of fitness or probity. The self-interested proponents of a new licensing law generally constitute a more effective political force than the citizens who, if aware of the matter at all, have no special interest which moves them to organize in opposition. The restrictive consequence of licensure is achieved in large part by making entry into the regulated occupation expensive in time and money or both.[44]

Professor Gellhorn concludes his observations about the abuse of licensing:

> [O]ccupational licensing has typically brought higher status for the producer of services at the price of higher costs to the consumer; it has reduced competition; it has narrowed opportunity for aspiring youth by increasing the cost of entry into a desired occupational career; . . . and it has caused a proliferation of official administrative bodies, most of them staffed by persons drawn from and devoted to furthering the interests of the licensed occupations themselves.[45]

Licensing and regulation reduce economic opportunities for people, especially those who might be described as discriminated against, those with little political clout, and latecomers.

CHAPTER 5

Excluding Blacks from Trades

One of the most significant things that I saw in the South — and I saw it everywhere — was the way in which white people were torn between their feelings of race prejudice and their downright economic needs.
—*Following the Color Line,* Ray Stannard Baker

THE UNITED STATES IS SEEN as a capitalist country. It has a history of both slavery and racial discrimination. Therefore, capitalism is frequently regarded as a system for the exploitation and mistreatment of black Americans. The degree to which our economic system is fully capitalistic need not distract us here. The question this chapter addresses is whether racism, in the sense of antipathy toward or personal preferences against blacks, by itself constitutes an insurmountable barrier to upward economic mobility. Considerable evidence suggests that racism by itself does not.

Using Licensing to Exclude Blacks

As discussed at length in Chapter 4, occupational licensing can reduce employment opportunities by creating artificial or unrealistic standards. It can occur without apparent racial motivation, as has been shown in the case of cosmetologists. Occupational licensing has also been used as a tool to achieve racist goals, such as the elimination of blacks from a craft. Historically, the tactic, when coupled with white-dominated craft unions, has been a particularly effective means of reducing black employment. Plumbers' and electricians' craft unions *explicitly* advocated licensure laws as a means to eliminate black competition. As Lorenzo Greene and Carter G. Woodson said, "A favorite method of barring [Negroes] from plumbing and electrical work was to install a system of unfair examinations which were conducted by whites."[1]

The following letter provides an example of one union's desire to eliminate black plumbers through licensure:

Editor Journal: Norfolk, Va.,
Dear Sir and Brother: February 12, 1905

Enclosed you will find a clipping from a Norfolk paper, which I would suggest that you give space in the next issue of the Journal, believing that it will be of interest to the members of U.A., especially of the southern district, as the Negro is a factor in this section, and I believe the enclosed Virginia state plumbing law which will eliminate him and the imposter from following our craft. . . .

(*Signed*) C. H. Perry, Sec. L.U.110[2]

Enclosed with the letter was a legislative bill containing the following commonly stated justification for the licensing of plumbers: "To promote the public health and to regulate the sanitary construction, house draining, and plumbing, and to secure the registration of plumbers in all cities. . . ."[3]

A Northern trade publication carried the following report:

. . . All the other work, jobbing, etc, is done by Negroes. . . . Bro. Becker and a few of the boys are going to run over to Greenville and make a thorough investigation and try to have these bosses hire white men. It is a wonder to me that there are not more Negroes working at our business from the way our members in a great many places use them as helpers. . . .[4]

The same issue of that publication contained this entry:

There are about ten Negro skate plumbers working around here [Danville, Virginia], doing quite a lot of jobbing and repairing, but owing to the fact of not having an examination board [licensing agency] it is impossible to stop them, hence the anxiety of the men here to organize.[5]

Proposals for licensing as a means of eliminating black tradesmen were not restricted to the South. In Kansas City, blacks were denied entry into a number of trades, including plumbing and electricity.[6] In New Jersey, it was reported to be impossible for a black to become a licensed plumber or steamfitter.[7] A study by Sterling D. Spero and Abraham L. Harris found that "in a city like Philadelphia, the licensing board will not grant a Negro a license—in Chicago the Negro plumbers have failed to gain advances after years of effort."[8]

Another method used to exclude, especially effective against blacks, involved apprenticeship examinations. Here are a few exam questions that, as late as 1968, a number of building trades unions used to screen candidates for their apprenticeship programs:

1. Czolgosz is to Booth as McKinley is to _____
   (a) Lincoln, (b) Washington, (c) Roosevelt, (d) Garfield.
2. Aztec is to Mexico as Maya is to _____
   (a) Peru, (b) Guatemala, (c) Haiti, (d) Uruguay.
3. _____ is to phlegmatic as vivacious is to _____ .
   (1) husky, (2) rheumatic, (3) pneumatic, (4) sluggish.
   (a) elusive, (b) pouting, (c) entertainer, (d) president.
4. _____ is to composer as Longfellow is to _____ .
   (1) Dali, (2) Van Gogh, (3) Riley, (4) Hayden.
   (a) musician, (b) poet, (c) entertainer, (d) president.
5. Revolution is related to evolution as flying is to _____ .
   (1) birds, (2) whirling, (3) walking, (4) wings, (5) standing.[9]

Typically, whites have attended higher-quality high schools than blacks and Hispanics. Such a test, whether intended to or not, will therefore disproportionately exclude the latter groups. It should go without saying that a capacity to answer questions such as those above have little to do with one's ability to be a plumber or carpenter.

Union Growth and Exclusion of Blacks from the Crafts

Blacks have not always been conspicuously absent or scarce in the skilled crafts and trades. Isaac Weld, in his eighteenth-century travels around the United States, observed that "Amongst their slaves are found tailors, shoemakers, carpenters, smiths, turners, wheelwrights, weavers, tanners, etc."[10]

Novelist James Weldon Johnson wrote, "The Negroes drove the horse and mule teams, they laid the bricks, they painted the buildings and fences, they loaded and unloaded ships. When I was a child, I did not know that there existed such a thing as a white carpenter or bricklayer or plasterer or tinner."[11]

According to Charles B. Rousseve: "Throughout the South where the majority of white men were too lazy to work, by far the largest proportion of labor, skilled and unskilled, was performed by Negroes, both freemen and the slave."[12] John Stephen Durham wrote about union exclusion of blacks from skilled crafts in the late 1800s:

> In the city of Washington, for example, at one period, some of the finest buildings were constructed by colored workmen. Their employment in large numbers continued some time after the war. The British Legation, the Centre Market, the Freeman's Bank, and at least four well-built schoolhouses are monuments to the acceptability of their work under foremen of their own color.
>
> Today, apart from hod-carriers, not a colored workman is to be seen on new buildings, and a handful of jobbers and patchers, with possibly two carpenters who can undertake a large job, are all who remain of the body of colored carpenters and builders and stone-cutters who were generally employed a quarter of a century ago.[13]

Commenting about stevedores, Durham said, "The effective organization of white laborers was closely followed by the driving of Negroes from the levees at the muzzles of loaded rifles. The iron industry is passing through the same experience. . . ."[14] Durham concluded, "[T]he real struggle of the unions is in opposition to the general desire of the employing class of the South to give the Negro whatever work he is capable of doing."[15]

Summarizing Durham's findings, Herbert Hill wrote: "Extending his inquiry into the North, Durham found the effects of the Negro exclusion policy to be even 'more manifest.'" In Philadelphia in 1838, the Society of Friends had compiled a directory of occupations in which Negroes were employed. Significantly included were such skilled jobs as cabinetmaker, plumber, printer, sailmaker, ship's carpenter, and stonecutter. By the end of the 1890s, Negroes had been forced out of most of these and other craft occupations.[16]

Hill continued his documentation of the impact of unions on Negro craft employment opportunities:

> In the older seaboard cities of the South, Negroes had once been employed in a great variety of occupations, skilled and unskilled. However, in the last decades of the nineteenth century the process of Negro displacement had begun, and trade unions were a most important part of this development. . . . In both South and North the trade union opposes black labor wherever it can and admits it to fellowship only as a last resort.[17]

It does not take much to conclude that the decline in black employment in the crafts, including electricians and plumbers, stemmed from a tradition of racial exclusion policies by labor unions. The International Brotherhood of Electrical Workers and the United Association of Plumbers and Steamfitters unions long excluded blacks from membership by tacit agreement among their members.[18] As of 1920, the Electrical Workers Union's 142,000 members included no blacks, even though there were 1,343 black electricians. Similarly, the Plumbers and Steamfitters Union included none of the 3,600 black plumbers among its membership of 35,000. Of the 6,000 black plasterers, the Plasterers Union had only 100 among its 30,000 members. The Sheet Metal Workers Union had no blacks among its 25,000 membership.[19]

In stark contrast to today, black leaders of the past were deeply suspicious about union motivation and recognized their harm and hostility to blacks. W. E. B. Dubois said, "[I]nstead of taking the part of the Negro and helping him toward physical and economic freedom, the America labor movement from the beginning has tried to achieve freedom at the expense of the Negro." Later he added, "The white employers, North and South, literally gave the Negroes work when white men refused to work with him; when he's scabbed for bread and butter the employers defended him against mob violence of white laborers; they gave him educational institutions when white labor would have left him in ignorance."[20]

Said Marcus Garvey, in urging blacks to undercut union wages as a means to employment and combating union racism, "the only convenient friend the Negro worker or laborer has in America at the present time is the white capitalist."[21] Similarly, in 1924, Howard University's Professor Kelly Miller urged blacks to "stand shoulder to shoulder with the captains of industry" in opposition to labor unions.[22] J. E. Bruce wrote that unions were a "greedy, grasping, ruthless, intolerant, overbearing, dictatorial combination of half-educated white men. . . . I am against them because they are against the Negro."[23] Both Frederick Douglass and Booker T. Washington were lifelong foes of unions.[24]

Some scholars have made the baseless argument that blacks earned the hostility of labor unions by their willingness to work for lower wages.[25] Unions could have easily fought this tendency by admitting blacks as members. Charles S. Johnson says that, "When the trade unions have been open to them, Negroes have entered as freely as white workers."[26] Others have asserted that blacks encountered union hostility because they allowed themselves to be used as strikebreakers.[27] This explanation overlooks the fact that strikebreaking was a necessary expedient because unions denied blacks membership. Johnson says:

> [M]any of the greatest advances which Negroes have made in industry, many of their first opportunities, are due to strikes and their part in breaking them. They were used to break the stockyard strike, and they have been employed there ever since; they were largely responsible for the failure of the steel strike, and they have been employed there ever since; and they now make up 17 percent of steel mill workers; they were used in the great railroad strike of 1922, and about 700 Negroes, mostly skilled, are still employed by one system alone. . . . The list could go on indefinitely.[28]

John G. Van Duesen was convinced that "criticism of the Negro strike-breaker comes with poor grace from unionists who subscribe to the policy of excluding Negroes from their Unions."[29]

Black and White Labor Violence

Labor violence in Chicago was a classic instance of racial competition in the labor market, and in 1919, it culminated in one of the nation's deadliest race riots.[30] When the riot was over, twenty-three blacks lay dead along with fifteen whites; well over 500 people of both races were injured. The history of Chicago's racial antagonism goes back to the Pullman strike of 1894, when packing and slaughterhouse workers struck in sympathy with Eugene V. Debs's American Railway Union. This strike marked the first time in the history of the packing industry that blacks were used as strikebreakers, and the action ended in defeat for the white workers.

In 1904, the packers once again went out on strike. This time the strike was over the skilled butchers' demand for a minimum wage of 20 cents an hour for their unskilled brethren, complaining that large packinghouses "began a system to crowd out the expert butchers and replace them by cheaper men in every way." They were displaced by "cheap Polackers and Hungarians. . . ."[31] As our earlier analysis of the economic effects of minimum wages would predict, "The skilled worker realized that this specialization enabled unskilled workers with 'muscle' to replace him; it appeared inevitable that unless a minimum wage were obtained for the unskilled, cut-throat job competition would drive all the wages down."[32]

Once again, the packers' strike was broken by blacks, who were hired as replacements by the thousands. And once again, they were subjected to extensive violence. Out of desperation as well as miscalculation, union leaders wired Booker T. Washington asking him to come to Chicago to lecture blacks on the subject: "Should Negroes Become Strikebreakers?" Washington turned the invitation down. South Carolina's Senator "Pitchfork Ben" Tillman, a rabid segregationist, came instead to tell the union workers, "It was the niggers that whipped you in line. . . . They were the club with which your brains were beaten out."[33]

In 1905, during a Chicago teamsters' strike, trainloads of black workers were brought in to deliver milk, coal, and other merchandise. They were set upon by angry strikers, and riots ensued. Chicago's city council enacted an order requesting that the city's corporation counsel file an opinion as to "whether the importation of hundreds of Negro workers is not a menace to the community and should be restricted." The employers' association responded by indicating a willingness not to import any more blacks, but refused to fire those already employed. The teamsters' president replied, "You have the Negroes in here to fight us and we answer that we have the right to attack them wherever found."

Indicative of white solidarity over strikebreaking was the sympathy strike conducted by hundreds of grade school students. They stoned black drivers delivering coal to their schools. Teachers and principals encouraged the students, in one case saying, "I invite the students to strike, if the dirty niggers deliver coal at this school."

Despite union and political pressure, employers continued to hire blacks—as more than temporary. According to an employer for Pullman Company, blacks were hired "not as strikebreakers, but with the understanding that their positions would be permanent," and they were "proving themselves much more efficient in every way than the cleaners who left. . . ." Labor competition benefited them. In 1910, Chicago's black population was 50,000; ten years later, it had doubled. During that period, the number of black workers in Chicago rose from 27,000 to 70,000. In the cattle shipping yards, their numbers rose from a mere 6 percent of the labor force to 32 percent. Black employment in every packinghouse increased by three to five times.[34]

Black newspapers and the Urban League understood the economics of the conflict, and took a conciliatory posture towards Chicago's racist unions saying, "We have arrayed ourselves on the side of capital to a great extent; yet capital has not played square with us; it has used us as strikebreakers, then when the calm came turned us adrift." Adding that if it were to the race's "economic, social and political interest to join with organized labor now, it should not make the least bit of difference what was their attitude toward us in the past, even if that past was as recent as yesterday. If they extend the olive branch in good faith accept it today."[35] Months later, after a convention of the American Federation of Labor (AFL), when its constituent unions did nothing to remove exclusion and segregation clauses, the *Chicago Defender* bitterly complained, "Unwillingly, we assume the role of strikebreakers. The unions drive us to it."[36] Black workers put their antipathy toward unions more forcefully: "Fuck the union, fuck you in the [union] button."

New Deal and Black Workers

While white unions could deny blacks membership, they were not as effective in denying them employment. Like any other seller of goods or services, black would-be workers found that they could appeal to employers' desire for higher profits through offering to work at lower prices. During the period of the "old" Supreme Court, frequently referred to as the Lochner era, laws that restricted freedom of contract and fostered monopolies were often struck down as unconstitutional violations of the "privileges and immunities" clauses of the Fifth and Fourteenth Amendments. That meant blacks (or any other less-preferred group, such as immigrants, women, and children) had a powerful weapon in coping with racial discrimination—the right to work for lower wages.

During the New Deal, the power of workers to offer that "compensating difference" began to erode. The National Recovery Act (NRA), which became law in 1933, established codes that required the payment of set wages for certain industries.[37] Those codes were established generally by exclusionary union-business panels. The NRA also provided for minimum wages based on what certain classes of workers received in the past. Since the act created set wages, it reduced employer incentives to hire blacks;[38] because such hiring provided no economic advantage, there was no reason for employers to put up with the white worker hostility and conflict that might result. Some employers dismissed black workers and hired whites in their place.[39] Others eliminated menial jobs held by blacks because they could not pay the mandated wage.

Section 7a of the NRA certified unions as exclusive bargaining agents. The NAACP's Roy Wilkins said that the AFL's strategy was to use section 7a "to organize a union for all workers, and to either agree with employers to push Negroes out of the industry or, having effected an agreement with the employer, proceed to make the union lily-white."[40] Black spokesmen and the black press were fully aware of the effects of the act. They referred to it variously as the "Negro Run Around," "Negroes Rarely Allowed," "Negroes Ruined Again," "Negroes Robbed Again," "No Roosevelt Again," and the "Negro Removal Act."[41] Professor Herbert Hill said that "the legislation intended to be the cornerstone of President Roosevelt's program to protect and uplift the working class had . . . become a millstone around the Black worker's neck."[42] In 1935, the U.S. Supreme Court ruled the NRA unconstitutional.[43] New Dealers mourned,[44] but the black community celebrated.[45]

The celebration was short-lived. In 1935, Section 7a of the NRA became Section 9 of the National Labor Relations Act (NLRA), popularly known as the Wagner Act, which established unions as the sole collective bargaining unit once the union became certified by the National Labor Relations Board (NLRB). The Wagner Act banned company unions and allowed unions to establish closed shops that had the power to bar non-members from employment. Originally, the Wagner Act contained a clause barring unions from discriminating against blacks. At the time, Howard University's Professor Miller predicted "the doom of the Negro in America industry if the Wagner Act did not contain a clause protecting blacks."[46] Under AFL political pressure, Senator Wagner dropped the anti-discrimination clause in order to retain union support and insure the act's passage.[47] Most New Dealers thought that discrimination against blacks was an acceptable and inevitable cost of economic recovery.[48]

The Wagner Act was widely thought to be unconstitutional;[49] however, the "new" Supreme Court, having abandoned judicial review of economic legislation, upheld its constitutionality.[50] This translated the unequal treatment of blacks by unions into a loss of previously available employment opportunities. In 1945, the NLRB made a face-saving ruling that a statutory bargaining agent must represent all employees fairly without regard to race.[51] However, the board also ruled that segregation and exclusion of blacks from union membership did not constitute an unfair labor practice. And it held that segregating blacks and whites into separate local unions was not a form of discrimination per se.[52]

New Deal legislation was clearly devastating for the black worker. In 1930, the national total unemployment rate was 6.13 percent. However, in that year, unemployment for blacks stood at 5.17 percent, almost a full percentage point below that for whites. 1930 was to be the last year a larger percentage of whites than of blacks would be unemployed.[53]

The Wagner Act not only conferred monopoly power on labor unions, it also made it illegal for employers to use blacks as strikebreakers. The higher, union-mandated wages led to mechanization and the elimination of some low-skilled jobs performed by blacks. The Agricultural Adjustment Act accelerated the mechanization of farms and displaced many black workers. In addition, the Fair Labor Standards Act, enacting minimum wages, began the elimination of many jobs and contributed to racial discrimination. As the renowned economist Gunnar Myrdal argued:

> When the jobs are made better, the employer becomes less eager to hire Negroes. There is, in addition, the possibility that the policy of setting minimum standards might cause some jobs to disappear altogether or to become greatly decreased. . . . If labor gets more expensive, it is likely to be economized and substituted for by machines. Also inefficient industries, which have hitherto existed solely by the exploitation of labor, may be put out of business when the government sets minimum standards.[54]

There is no question about racist union exclusionary policy and practices of the past. But what can be said about today? There is little evidence of continued flagrant racial exclusion. However, in some craft unions, blacks are virtually absent. That can be explained in several interrelated ways. One is that black workers may not be seeking to join the union because, seeing the relatively few black members, they view their chances of admission as slim. Second, entry requirements may have been raised to discourage black membership. That, related to a third possible reason, is the entire package of entry conditions, which includes long apprenticeship periods and restrictions on the number of apprentices, seniority rules, artificially high wages, and licensure. Regardless of whether unions discriminate racially today, all these union-supported practices tend to discriminate against lower-skilled tradesmen.

Black Opportunity Nowadays in Electrical and Plumbing Work

Racial discrimination by occupational licensing boards is not just a historical curiosity made irrelevant by racial enlightenment of today. In 1973, Benjamin Shimberg reported:

> The only licensed Negro plumber in Montgomery County, Alabama, at the time of this study reported that he had spent four years learning the plumbing trade at Talladega College, but that when he attempted to obtain a license, he faced seemingly insurmountable barriers. He took the local examination and was told each time that he failed. He was not told what his score was nor was he allowed to see his examination paper. Finally he took and passed the state master plumber's examination and then managed to use his state license as a means of obtaining a local license in Montgomery County.[55]

Professor Shimberg added that black electricians faced similar difficulty in Alabama. Union-sponsored electrical apprenticeship programs appear closed to them. The union requirement is that all applicants must be high school graduates. High school-equivalency test certificates are not accepted. Final selection to the apprenticeship training programs is determined on the basis of a personal interview, which affords considerable latitude for racial discrimination.[56]

Shimberg insightfully points out that the vested economic interests that are protected from competition by state licensing boards cannot be persuaded to change their practices voluntarily: ". . . nor is there much room for optimism that many state legislatures or city councils would be willing to incur the wrath of powerful labor unions or affluent trade associations whose members derive economic benefits from the perpetuation of the status quo."[57]

According to Equal Employment Opportunity Commission data, blacks in 1969 constituted 1.9 percent of the membership of the International Brotherhood of Electrical Workers (IBEW) and 0.6 percent of the United Association of Plumbers and Pipefitters.[58] By 1972, their membership had risen to 6.5 percent and 4.4 percent, respectively.[59] In a study of the "mechanical" trades (boilermakers, electrical workers, elevator constructors, ironworkers, plumbers and pipefitters, and sheet metal workers), Herbert Hammerman found that in 1972, 58 percent of the local unions had no black or Spanish-origin members.[60]

While the number of black union members is not a perfect measure of racial discrimination, it does suggest that licensing and unionization had an ongoing, adverse impact on minority opportunities to become plumbers and electricians. The issue of occupational entry barriers, imposed by state licensing authorities or by labor organizations, is not whether open racial discrimination is practiced. The issue, as far as policy is concerned, is the barriers' racial effect.

There is evidence that occupational licensing is used in other ways that handicap minorities. This happens when incumbent practitioners attempt to protect their income in the face of a slack market for their services. Professor Alex Maurizi investigated the relationships, in licensed occupations, between a slack market for labor and the examination pass rate.[61] He found that a substantial, statistically significant portion of the pass rate was explained by the excess demand. When there was high unemployment in the licensed trade, the examination increased in difficulty in order to reduce the number of new entrants and, by extension, protect the incomes of incumbent practitioners. Obviously, that will have the greatest discriminatory impact on the groups that have a poorer-quality education; minorities disproportionately comprise such groups.

Blacks and the Railroad Industry

Despite the fact that the railroad industry has historically been the source of some of the most virulent forms of racial discrimination, at the turn of the century, thousands of blacks found employment on America's railroads.[62] A number of railroad unions had constitutional provisions banning them from membership. Among those were the Switchmen's Union of North America and numerous "Brotherhoods": Railway Carmen, Railway Conductors, Railway Clerks, Locomotive Firemen and Enginemen, and Maintenance-of-Way Employees. Blacks were also banned from other unions with railroad workers among their members—the International Association of Machinists, the Boilermakers, the Iron Shipbuilders and Helpers Union.[63]

Although unions were able to bar blacks from membership, they could not bar them from the craft itself. In fact, in the South, where hostility toward black workmen was the greatest, some railroad companies had firemen crews that were 85 to 90 percent black. For Southern states as a whole, blacks constituted 27 percent of the brakemen and 12 percent of the switchmen. Those numbers changed radically in later years. By 1940, only 18 percent of the firemen in the South were blacks, falling to 7 percent by 1960.[64] W. E. B. Dubois, writing of this era, concluded, "The great railway systems too discriminate against the Negro, and here his opportunity is limited, no matter how high a degree of efficiency he may attain, to the menial and poorly paid tasks."[65]

Table 5.1 illustrates the number of black and white firemen by years and region. It shows a drop in the total number of firemen both by year and region since 1920. But most remarkable is the decline in the number of black firemen—compared to whites—after that date. The falloff in that specialty was the greatest in the South, where at one time they were the most numerous.

The high rate of employment for blacks in the railroad industry resulted not from white benevolence but because blacks would work for wages that were often just two-thirds of those paid to white firemen for doing the same job. The wage differential had the clear effect of reducing the power of white firemen to demand higher wages. As one white fireman put it, "Every time the firemen ask for an increase in wages or for overtime due them, they are told by the superintendent, 'Why, I can get a Negro in your place for one dollar, while I'm paying you $1.50 per day.'"[66]

Railroad companies were very much interested in keeping blacks in their employ because hiring blacks meant lower operating costs. White firemen naturally protested, alleging black incompetence, but also resorted to large-scale, crippling strikes, intimidation, and even murder.

Union Demands for Equal Pay

In 1909, a bitter strike took place against the Georgia Railroad. The Brotherhood of Locomotive Firemen demanded that blacks be completely eliminated from the railroad. Instead of recommending that, the arbitration board decided that black firemen, hostlers, and hostlers' helpers must be

Table 5.1. Locomotive Firemen in the United States by Region, 1910–60 (Males Only)

Region		1910 White	1910 Black	1920 White	1920 Black	1930 White	1930 Black	1940 White	1940 Black	1950 White	1950 Black	1960 White	1960 Black
South	Number	14,755	5,012	17,722	5,878	14,309	4,254	9,545	2,114	12,690	1,823	9,563	750
	Percent	(74.6)	(25.4)	(75.1)	(24.9)	(77.1)	(22.9)	(81.9)	(18.1)	(87.4)	(12.6)	(92.7)	(7.3)
	Number Change	—	—	2,967	866	-3,413	-1,624	-4,764	-2,140	3,145	-291	-3,127	-1,073
	Percent Change	—	—	20.1	17.3	-19.3	-27.6	-33.3	-50.3	32.9	-13.8	-24.6	-58.9
North-Central	Number	28,353	105	32,762	359	23,814	234	15,430	88	20,063	250	13,925	62
	Percent	(99.6)	(.4)	(98.9)	(1.1)	(99.0)	(1.0)	(99.4)	(.6)	(98.8)	(1.2)	(99.6)	(.4)
	Number Change	—	—	4,409	254	-8,948	-125	-8,384	-146	4,633	162	-6,138	-188
	Percent Change	—	—	15.5	241.9	-27.3	-34.8	-35.2	-62.4	30.0	184.1	-30.6	-75.2
North-East	Number	19,202	53	24,765	217	17,128	138	11,341	54	12,080	123	7,545	33
	Percent	(99.7)	(.3)	(99.1)	(.9)	(99.2)	(.8)	(99.5)	(.5)	(99.0)	(1.0)	(99.6)	(.4)
	Number Change	—	—	5,563	164	-7,637	-79	-5,787	-84	739	69	-4,535	-90
	Percent Change	—	—	29.0	309.4	-30.8	-36.4	-33.8	-60.9	6.5	127.8	-37.5	-73.2
West	Number	8,883	18	9,611	31	6,122	14	5,258	7	6,872	26	5,071	5
	Percent	(99.8)	(.2)	(99.7)	(.3)	(99.8)	(.2)	(99.9)	(.1)	(99.6)	(.4)	(99.9)	(.1)
	Number Change	—	—	728	13	-3,489	-17	-864	-7	1,614	19	-1,081	-21
	Percent Change	—	—	8.2	72.2	-36.3	-54.8	-14.1	-50.0	30.7	271.4	-26.2	-80.8

Sources: Department of Commerce, Bureau of the Census, *Census of the Population: 1910*, vol. 2, Occupations, table 2 (Washington, D.C.: Government Printing Office, 1910); *Census: 1920*, vol. 4, Occupations, table 15, 66; *Census: 1930*, vol. 4, Occupations by State, table 11; *Census: 1940*, vol. 3, The Labor Force, table 63, 91; *Census: 1950*, vol. 2, pt. 1, Detailed Characteristics, table 139, 1–397; *Census: 1960*, vol. 1, pt. 1D, Detailed Characteristics, table 257, 717; *Census, Negro Population: 1790–1915*, Occupation Table, table 17, 517–20; *Census: 1920*, vol. 4, Occupations, Ch. 7, table 1, 874–1,048.

paid wages that *equaled* the wages of whites doing the same job.[67] Although that move did not meet its demand, the union expressed delight, saying, "If this course is followed by the company and the incentive for employing Negroes thus removed, the strike will not have been in vain."[68]

Why would the Locomotive Firemen be happy with the decision for equal pay for equal work? Because if railroads were required to pay blacks the same as they paid whites, the cost to the railroad of discriminating against blacks in employment would in effect be zero. The pay rule would effectively prevent blacks from competing with whites by offering to work for lower wages. White firemen knew that well. They also knew that they could trust economic incentives to further their racist objectives better than custom, gentlemen's agreements, or feelings of white solidarity.

White understanding of the power of wage regulation to further the cause of racial discrimination in employment is evident in an agreement between the Brotherhood of Railway Trainmen and the Southern Railroad Association signed in Washington, D.C., in January 1910. The agreement read in part:

> No larger percentage of Negro firemen or yardmen will be employed in any division or in any yard than was employed on January 1, 1910. If on any roads this percentage is now larger than on January 1, 1910, this agreement does not contemplate the discharge of any Negroes to be replaced by whites; but as vacancies are filled or new men employed, whites are to be taken until the percentage of January first is again reached. Negroes are not to be employed as baggage men, flagmen or yard foremen, but in any case in which they are so now employed, they are not to be discharged to make places for whites, but when the positions they occupy become vacant, whites shall be employed in their places.
>
> *Where no difference in the rates of pay between white and colored exists, the restrictions as to percentage of Negroes to be employed does not apply.*[69]

In other words, white firemen insisted on hard and fast quotas for the hiring of blacks when there was no wage regulation. They recognized that openly discriminatory measures were not needed if wages between the races were equal. They perhaps also realized that if they insisted on racial quotas where wages were equal, blacks might have employment opportunities that otherwise would not be available.

Firemen's brotherhoods, fresh from their victory over Southern railroads, followed up by negotiating a similar discriminatory agreement with the railroads in the Mississippi Valley. These agreements, with the full backing of government and monopolistic labor laws, led to the virtual elimination of blacks from all but the industry's most menial jobs. Railroad companies were coerced and blackmailed into not hiring blacks as a condition for labor peace.

Efforts to eliminate black railroad employment often resulted in the use of violence. In a 1911 strike against the Cincinnati, New Orleans and Texas Pacific Railroad protesting the employment of blacks, ten black firemen were murdered.[70] The strike resulted in an agreement by which the railroad would not hire blacks north of certain geographical boundaries.[71] In some cases, black workers were beaten, kidnapped, and murdered for refusing to leave the job.[72] Herbert Hill describes other violent incidents in Texas and Georgia following union petitions to replace black workers with whites.[73]

The fact that blacks found employment opportunities on America's rails had little or nothing to do with white employer benevolence. One doubts whether there were systemic racial preference differences between whites who were employers and whites who were workers. The reason is much simpler. Blacks simply underbid whites for the jobs, i.e., they were willing to sell their labor services at lower prices. Railroad owners were more interested in higher profits than in white solidarity.

The Use of the State Against Blacks

Early U.S. Supreme Court decisions thwarted union attempts to exclude black workers. *In re Debs* upheld a federal injunction against Eugene V. Debs's whites-only American Railway Union, which sought to monopolize the labor market.[74] Courts often issued injunctions enforcing "yellow-dog" contracts, wherein workers, as a condition of employment, agreed not to join a union. Pressured by labor unions, Congress enacted a statute banning interstate railroads from enforcing those contracts.[75] In 1908, in *Adair v. United States,* the Supreme Court overturned the statute as a violation of the freedom of contract.[76] In *Coppage v. Kansas* (1915), the court struck down state bans on yellow-dog contracts involving *intra*state railroads.[77] That decision hampered the unions' ability to use state legislatures in their efforts to remove black workers.

Blacks recognized the importance of yellow-dog contracts implied in the freedom to contract for their services. In testimony before the Senate Judiciary Committee, during the Shipstead anti-injunction hearings in 1928, Harry E. Davis, a black politician from Ohio, said, "It logically follows that a colored worker who is denied the protection and benefits of organized labor because they will not take him in, has only one place of redress in case his right of employment is assailed and that is in our courts. . . ." Davis went on to say, "The group I represent has not got very much physical or tangible property, and their biggest asset is their right to a job, recognized as a contract, but an intangible right, and I maintain that if this bill becomes a law, it would affect very materially their right to the biggest thing which they have, a right to earn a living."[78]

The New Deal and Black Railroad Workers

What racially discriminatory railroad labor unions could not accomplish through intimidation, collective bargaining, and earlier court decisions, they were able to accomplish through New Deal legislation. Primary among this legislation was the Railway Labor Act (RLA) of 1926, as amended in 1934.[79] The RLA provided that "The majority of any craft or class of employees shall have the right to determine who shall be the representative of the class or craft. . . ."[80] The act forced employers to negotiate with certified union representatives supporting worker rights to contract freely. Despite previous U.S. Supreme Court decisions, it also outlawed yellow-dog contracts and company unions. In addition, the RLA also created the National Mediation Board (NMB) and the National Railroad Adjustment Board (NRAB), giving the former jurisdiction over union certification and the latter jurisdiction over disputes arising from collective bargaining agreements.

Nearly all railroad unions banned black membership by constitutional provisions.[81] Blacks who were not accepted for membership in most locals, or were relegated to a low status in the railroad unions, naturally attempted to form their own unions. Those attempts were nullified by the action of the NRAB, which simply ruled that these alternative unions, created by workers discriminated against, could not represent black employees who were being unfairly represented by the bargaining unit given exclusive rights by the board. In effect, the board bestowed monopoly representation powers on white labor unions that refused equal membership terms to blacks.

The adverse effects of this policy stand out in stark relief in the 1943 case of *Brotherhood of Railway and Steamship Clerks v. United Transport Service Employees of America* (UTSEA).[82] The court in this case was asked to settle the conflicting claims of two unions competing for the rights to represent forty-five black porters at a train station in St. Paul, Minnesota. The porters were ineligible for membership in the Brotherhood of Railway and Steamship Clerks Union because they were black; they unanimously voted for UTSEA as their bargaining agent. The NMB dismissed the application of UTSEA on the grounds that the porters were not a separate class of employees and that there was no dispute over representation. A court held that the Brotherhood of Railway and Steamship Clerks, which banned black membership, represented all porters, both black and white.

A federal district court declared the NMB dismissal order void. On appeal, an appellate court pointed out that the dismissal of UTSEA's right to represent black employees forced them to accept representation by an organization in which they had no right to membership or right to speak or be heard on their own behalf. Yet the black workers' victory was not to be had: the U.S. Supreme Court reversed the appellate decision on the ground that the mediation board's certifications are not subject to judicial review.[83] During this era and later, numerous certification proceedings granted racially discriminatory labor unions exclusive bargaining representation.[84]

The discriminatory practices of railway labor unions, reinforced by national labor laws, gave rise to several other important court cases. Chief among them was *Steele v. Louisville & Nashville Railroad.*[85] It involved a black fireman, B. W. Steele, who had been laid off as a result of the Southeastern Carrier's Agreement, a pact among several railroad companies and railway labor organizations. Steele and three other blacks had been working as firemen in the high-paying passenger division of the Louisville & Nashville line. The union had declared the jobs of the four blacks vacant, and they were later filled by white firemen having less seniority.

When Steele first started working as a fireman in 1910, 98 percent of the firemen in his Louisville & Nashville district were black. By 1943, the proportion had dropped to 20 percent. Steele's case was originally brought before the Alabama supreme court, which found that, as a certified representative of the firemen, the railway brotherhood had the right to destroy or create rights of members of the bargaining unit.[86] However, in 1944, when the U.S. Supreme Court heard the case, it reversed the state court decision and found that the union had violated the Railway Labor Act. In reaching its decision, the Court recognized that the RLA would be on very weak constitutional grounds if it denied individuals *both* the right to bargain for themselves and the right to be fairly represented by the exclusive bargaining unit. The Court ruled that "the Railway Labor Act imposes on the bargaining representative of a craft or class of employees the duty to exercise fairly the power conferred upon it in behalf of all those for whom it acts, without hostile discrimination against them."[87]

Yet, despite that finding, effective discrimination against black railroad workers did not end. The mechanism for its continuance had not been weakened—namely, the monopoly powers conferred upon unions by the federal government. The Brotherhood of Locomotive Firemen ignored the Court's decision and maintained the illegal Southeastern Carrier's Agreement. Not until the 1950s, following separate lawsuits awarding damages, did the effect of the *Steele* decision become even modestly felt.[88]

In the 1940s, unions began to employ subtler discriminatory techniques that had the effect of reducing or eliminating black firemen. For example, the Brotherhood of Locomotive Firemen began a campaign that, at least superficially, appeared to be aimed at rejecting its racially discriminatory practices of the past by negotiating an agreement that struck out the anti-black-quota clause. The brotherhood proposed to the members of the Southeastern Carrier's Conference a test to determine whether a fireman was promotable. Failing the test after three tries would mean that the man was not promotable and would be dismissed.

Obviously, the test was directed at eliminating black firemen. Most of them had been hired many years ago, when education requirements did not exist. The test based on the hiring requirement for engineers would have caused the blacks to be dismissed as unpromotable. Fortunately for the firemen around the country, the U.S. Supreme Court held that the test was illegal.[89]

Charles Houston, who was the lawyer for many black railway men, points out how the federal government failed to protect blacks and actually colluded with their oppressors. For example, government officials permitted white unions to assist in writing the 1934 Railway Labor Act. Furthermore, each union brotherhood had its representative sitting on the section of the National Railroad Adjustment Board that held jurisdiction over all grievances affecting train and engine service employment.[90]

Racist Union Policy Toward Others: A Digression

Samuel Gompers, the first president of the AFL, is mistakenly revered by many as the benevolent father of the labor movement. He is seen as not having a single racist bone in his body. But he warned, "Caucasians are not going to let their standard of living be destroyed by Negroes, Chinamen, Japs or any other."[91]

Gompers held particular animosity against Orientals. In 1906, the AFL called for immigration restrictions; although he himself had immigrated from Poland, Gompers declared that "the maintenance of the nation depended upon the maintenance of racial purity and strength."[92] The most comprehensive statement of his feelings about Orientals is found in a pamphlet that he coauthored with Herman Gutstat, another AFL official: "Some Reasons for Chinese Exclusion: Meat vs. Rice, American Manhood Against Coolieism—Which Shall Survive."[93] According to the authors, the Chinese were congenitally immoral: "The Yellow man found it natural to lie, cheat and murder and ninety-nine out of one hundred Chinese are gamblers." Gompers said Chinese were good workers in American households, but "he [the Chinese individual] goes joyfully back to his slum and his burrow to the grateful luxury of his normal surroundings—vice, filth, and an atmosphere of horror."[94]

In 1883, answering questions put to him by the chairman of the Senate Committee on Education and Labor, Gompers stated union policy toward the Chinese:

A. I have no objection to the people of any country coming to America, Chinese excepted (I'm not so sentimental as all that), provided they come here of their own free will, and not influenced by deception.

Q. On that point, do you think there is any feeling among American laborers or workmen adverse to free and open competition with foreign laborers from European countries when they come here?

A. No, sir; I believe they have no objection. They do wish, however, to put a stop to the introduction of the Chinese into this country, at least for a period, so as to give the American workman a breathing spell. Our people had hardly recovered from the Panic and they were not to be trodden down by the Chinese undermining them.

Q. But a European laborer will work more cheaply than the American laborer, will he not?

A. He becomes easily acclimatized and soon harmonizes with the American people.

Q. And he soon wants as much wages as anybody?

A. Yes, sir; and, as a certain senator said, "It is a question whether the working men of America shall eat rats, rice, or beefsteak." I choose beefsteak. I will vote for that every time. I do not want it understood that my vote can be purchased for a beefsteak, but I will vote always for measures that will improve the condition of the working men."

Q. You speak of this opposition to the Chinese being designed to give the working men a breathing spell after the Panic. Do I understand you to mean that the opposition to Chinese immigration is temporary?

A. No, sir.

Q. Then, there is a permanent opposition, you think to that immigration?

A. Decidedly.[95]

In other speeches, letters and writings, Gompers and other high union officials made it clear that similar feelings, and subsequent union practices, extended to Japanese, Koreans, and Mexican-Americans.[96]

Racial Discrimination in the Trucking Industry

The discriminatory practices of the International Brotherhood of Teamsters, the dominant union in trucking, have been an important impediment to black opportunities in the industry. Unions played a major role in excluding blacks from trucking, particularly in the South. In the post-Civil War days, it was regarded as a "Negro job." As wages in the industry began to rise, however, the job became attractive to whites. And as the trucking industry became more unionized, union work rules penalized blacks trying to advance to the more lucrative position of over-the-road driver.

The International Brotherhood of Teamsters negotiated seniority rules that were part of its National Master Freight Agreement. Although there were blacks in the section of the Teamsters Union that dealt in over-the-road labor, those drivers were on a separate seniority list. The significance of that: if a dockman or a local driver sought to move to the over-the-road list, he had to give up all the seniority rights he held and go to the bottom of the over-the-road seniority list. Such a rule, because of the risks of unemployment and layoffs, acted as a powerful inducement not to transfer. As pointed out by attorney William B. Gould,[97] this form of seniority rules was unlawful to the extent that they adversely affect minorities.[98] According to Gould, "[N]o matter how many courts declared the provisions unlawful, the parties not directly ordered to make changes continued to adhere to the same practices and procedures."[99] He argued that discriminatory seniority rules continued because (1) the Teamsters were a highly decentralized organization and (2) the government had been unwilling to carry its confrontation with the trucking industry to a showdown. Union officials threatened a nationwide strike if any company hired a black because of government pressure.

The economic impact of seniority rules struck through collective bargaining agreements was critical: they reduced minority opportunities to gain over-the-road trucking skills. They also perpetuated the effects of past discrimination, because many trucking companies did not hire black road drivers until more recent times.[100] Teamster locals often demanded that trucking companies practice racial employment discrimination against blacks as a condition for labor peace.[101]

Another significant factor in the problem that blacks faced in getting over-the-road truck driving positions was the refusal of white truck drivers to ride with them. In 1966, *The Wall Street Journal* reported that one Teamster official asked, "Would you like to climb in a bunk bed that a nigger just got out of?" Another said, "To my knowledge no law has been written yet that says a white man has to bed down with Negroes."[102] Teamster officials protected union men who were discharged by a company for refusing to ride with a black driver.[103]

Seniority rules, the refusal of white drivers to ride with black drivers, and the Teamsters' highly discriminatory job-referral practices contributed to reducing black opportunities for jobs in the trucking industry.[104]

Deregulation and Black Opportunities

Traditionally, blacks have had few opportunities in the trucking industry, working either as for-hire drivers or owner-operators. There is little evidence that discrimination in the trucking industry came to an end after passage of the Civil Rights Act of 1964, with its Title VII making employment discrimination illegal. It nonetheless persisted against blacks, reinforced by the fact that for new hires, trucking firms relied primarily on either union or driver referrals. The use of newspaper ads or employment agencies, which might have attracted black applicants, was largely nonexistent.[105]

The story changed after deregulation. Taking 1979 as the beginning of trucking deregulation, a commentator noted at the time that "the portion of blacks working in the traditionally lucrative for-hire sector increases to 27 percent from a regulated period of 21 percent. . . . Blacks appear to be more likely to be hired in the for-hire sector following deregulation than before."[106] Also after deregulation, a larger percentage of blacks became union members.[107]

Deregulating the industry opened up opportunities for black owner-operators. "Of the minority certifications in force in mid–1981, 48 percent had been granted between the commission's creation earlier in the century and deregulation in 1978. The other 52 percent had been granted in the two and one-half years following deregulation."[108] During the regulated period, only 9.4 percent of the Current Population Survey (CPS) sample were owner-operators; after deregulation, blacks accounted for 26.4 percent of

Table 5.2. Minority-Owned Common Carriers

State	1983	1992	State	1983	1992
Alabama	4	10	Montana	1	5
Alaska	4	1	Nebraska	3	4
Arizona	5	12	Nevada	4	2
Arkansas	1	6	New Hampshire	1	1
California	92	142	New Jersey	29	68
Canada	2	4	New Mexico	5	18
Colorado	4	14	New York	16	44
Connecticut	2	11	North Carolina	13	46
Delaware	1	7	North Dakota	1	3
District Of Columbia	7	4	Ohio	12	23
Florida	17	48	Oklahoma	6	15
Georgia	5	29	Oregon	7	17
Hawaii	1	Not Available	Pennsylvania	6	19
Idaho	5	8	Rhode Island	Not Available	3
Illinois	20	39	South Carolina	2	15
Indiana	7	11	South Dakota	6	1
Iowa	Not Available	4	Tennessee	5	16
Kansas	4	7	Texas	17	98
Kentucky	1	6	Utah	1	Not Available
Louisiana	4	16	Vermont	0	Not Available
Maine	3	1	Virginia	14	28
Maryland	24	32	Washington	7	15
Massachusetts	9	10	West Virginia	1	2
Michigan	16	30	Wisconsin	2	6
Minnesota	5	10	Wyoming	1	
Missouri	5	6			
Mississippi	2	19	**Total**	**410**	**936**

Source: Motor Carrier Listings, Minority and Female, Office of Public Assistance (Washington, D.C.: Office of Transportation Analysis, Interstate Commerce Commission, September 1983 and April 1993).

that category. By comparison, blacks were three times more likely after deregulation to be owner-operators than they were before it.[109] A study by John S. Heywood and James H. Peoples supports the economic prediction that deregulation and its resulting competition reduced the scope for discrimination.[110]

Table 5.2 shows, as of 1992, the number of minority-owned common carriers with certificates of authority from the Interstate Commerce Commission (ICC). The listing does not determine what percentage of those is black-owned versus other minorities. However, it does suggest a significant surge in minority ownership of freight- and passenger-transportation companies *since* deregulation. In 1981, there were approximately 314 minority carriers among the 22,000 carriers subject to ICC regulations.[111] By 1992, as shown in Table 5.2, that number had grown to 936.

Another result of the Motor Carrier Act of 1980, which deregulated the interstate trucking industry, was a near-doubling of the number of authorized ICC carriers: they rose from 18,000 in 1980 to 33,548 in 1984. During the first year of deregulation alone, the commission granted authorization for 27,960 additional routes to new and existing carriers. Freight rates fell between 5 percent and 20 percent during 1980 and 1981. By 1986, revenue per truckload fell by 22 percent.[112] The reason: greater competition brought more schedule reliability and more specialization of services. Failure rates were greater after deregulation, but truck efficiency and accident rates improved

The squeeze on profits forced less efficient firms out of the market. Prior to deregulation, restrictive entry and price-fixing enabled inefficient producers to survive.[113]

Conclusion

Our short discussion of the trucking industry before and after deregulation offers additional confirmation of our working hypothesis that government regulations close avenues of entry and reinforce economic handicaps. Deregulation has not only served to help minorities enter an industry in greater numbers; it has also benefited consumers through lower prices and greater convenience in securing services.

Deregulation has been valuable in another important way. It has increased black participation in the trucking industry without depending upon controversial measures that have caused so much divisiveness in our society, namely quotas and racial preferences. Many people see those remedies as a violation of democratic principles. However, implicit in the criticism of them is the assumption that the economic game is being played fairly, that it is open to all with the will and means to enter.

In many instances, as demonstrated by the history of the trucking industry, the game was not fair. Through ICC regulation, it was rigged in a way particularly devastating to blacks. A moral dilemma therefore arose and persists: if we retain various laws and regulations that systematically mitigate against black opportunities, what should be done? If we retain these restrictive laws and regulations, maybe a case can be made for racial preferences as a "second-best" solution. The "first-best" solution, in terms of equity, efficiency, and morality, is to eliminate restrictive laws and regulations. When this course is pursued, it ameliorates the injustice *and* brings the side benefit of doing so without the rancor and divisiveness of racial remedies.

Whether one is dealing with licensure laws, wage legislation, or economic regulation, racial discrimination alone does not sufficiently explain entry restrictions. They are more an issue between the ins and the outs. Timothy Person, a black CEO of the St. Louis, Missouri-based Allstates Transworld Van Lines, struggled for thirty years with the ICC in an effort to achieve nationwide authority to ship household goods. The struggle cost him more than $1 million in expenses and lost profits. But in 1980, his efforts paid off, making his the first black firm—and one of only nineteen eventually—to achieve nationwide certification. That meant a huge boost to his revenue. Given Person's struggles with the ICC and its regulations, one might be tempted to think that he would like to see less regulation in the household-goods shipping industry. But that is not the case. He sees government regulation as necessary to protect the consumer.

He said, "It would have been foolhardy of me to have spent the time and money and energy to get the national license if I had believed that regulation was going to turn [other] truckers loose on the public."[114] Person's interests had become the same as that of other shipping companies with nationwide certification—namely, restrictions on entry as a means to greater wealth.

CHAPTER 6

Racial Terminology and Confusion

Error is never so difficult to be destroyed as when
it has roots in language.
—Jeremy Bentham, *On Evidence*

WITHOUT A DOUBT, part of the confusion in understanding racial issues lies in the imprecise and ambiguous language used by scholars and laymen alike in discussing race. Words can, and usually do, have more than one meaning, and therefore can be used ambiguously. In analytical usage, not only is it necessary to separate the connotative from the literal content of words, but precise and operationally useful distinctions and definitions also must be made.

An example of ambiguous language is found in the use of the phrase "racial segregation." Consider the following observations. Blacks represent about 65 percent of the Washington, D.C., population. Reagan National Airport serves the Washington area, and like every such facility, it has water fountains. At no time has the writer observed anything close to blacks being 65 percent of water fountain users; a wild guess would place their usage at 5 or 10 percent at most. To the extent that this observation approximates reality, would anyone move to declare that Reagan airport water fountains are racially segregated?

Casual observation of ice hockey games would suggest that blacks attend them far below their percentages in the general population. A similar observation can be made about operas, dressage performances, and wine tastings. The population statistics of states such as South Dakota, Iowa,

Maine, Montana, and Vermont show that not even 1 percent of their populations is black. On the other hand, in states such as Georgia, Alabama, and Mississippi, blacks are overrepresented in terms of their percentage in the general population. Would anyone suggest that racial segregation accounts for any of those observations?

Just because blacks are not proportionately represented in some activity, according to their numbers in the general population, how analytically useful is it to assert that the activity is racially segregated? A more useful test is whether, for example, a black person at Reagan airport is free to drink from any water fountain he chooses. If the answer is in the affirmative, then the water fountains are not racially segregated, and that would be true even if no black person ever uses the water fountains.

If the average American were asked whether the country's public schools are segregated, a consensus would be virtually impossible. Some would argue, as has Harvard University's Civil Rights Project, that schools *are* racially segregated and becoming more so:

> Civil rights goals have not been accomplished. The country has been going backward toward greater segregation in all parts of the country for more than a decade. Since the end of the Civil Rights era, there has been no significant leadership towards the goal of creating a successfully integrated society built on integrated schools and neighborhoods.[1]

A little reflection on the matter shows that people give the term racial segregation one meaning when applied to water fountains, operas, and ice hockey games—and an entirely different meaning when applied to schools and neighborhoods. The test used to determine whether Reagan airport water fountains were segregated or not should also be used to answer the question of whether schools were segregated or not. If a black student lives within a particular school district, is he free to attend that school? If the answer is affirmative, then the schools are not segregated, even if not a single black attends the school. In contrast to the past, there are today no legal or extra-legal barriers to keep blacks who reside within a school district from attending its schools.

When an activity is not racially mixed today, a better word is racially homogeneous, which does not mean that it is racially segregated, at least in the historic usage of the term. It would surely be deemed ridiculous, foolhardy, and a gross abuse of government power if, for example, one were to conclude that since blacks are "underrepresented" at Reagan airport water fountains, there ought to be a policy to bus blacks to such fountains. Similarly, I doubt whether one would propose compelling blacks to move from Georgia to Iowa, and the reverse for whites, until those actions satisfied some sort of preconceived notion of what constitutes racial integration across states. Why blacks are "underrepresented" in some activities and "overrepresented" in others may reflect personal preferences, history, cultural influences, income differences, and discrimination.

Those who advocate and litigate for school desegregation today are not fighting against state and local laws that mandate racial separation. Their argument rests solely on the fact that black attendance at some schools is not proportional to or representative of the numbers of blacks in the population. For those advocates and litigators, the school does not have a pleasing racial mix. The fact that many of today's large-city school systems are predominantly black is mostly a result of residential housing patterns and not legislated school-segregation policy. That fact makes racial heterogeneity virtually impossible. For example, in Manhattan, public schools are nearly 90 percent black or Hispanic, while private schools are 80 percent white.

While there is a smaller overall percentage of blacks in private schools, they are somewhat more racially heterogeneous nowadays. Those who see racial heterogeneity in schools as desirable should support measures such as education vouchers or tuition tax credits to strengthen the private-education sector. A majority of black parents support educational vouchers that would allow them educational choice.[2]

Other terms and concepts used in the racial literature and debate are just as misleading and confusing. Among the aims of this chapter is to discuss those ambiguities, suggest operational definitions, and maybe shed more light on racial phenomena we observe.

Discrimination Operationally Defined

More generally, and inclusive of legal attempts to define the term, discrimination might be operationally defined as the act of choice or selection. All selection necessarily and simultaneously requires *non*-selection. Choice requires discrimination. When one chooses to attend the University of

Chicago, he non-selects or discriminates against Harvard University as well as every other university. When one selects a Bordeaux wine, he non-selects a Burgundy wine. We might call these cases university discrimination and wine discrimination. Similarly, when the term discrimination is modified with the nouns race and sex, we merely specify the criterion upon which the choice is made.

At this juncture, we might ask if there is any conceptual distinction between discriminating for or against particular universities, wines, and other goods and services and discriminating for or against particular races and sexes. Or should one discriminate at all? Can one make a case for indifference or random choice among universities, wine, or people? Indifference or random choice is hardly ever the case. Our lives are largely spent discriminating for or against prospective selected activities, objects, and people. Some of us discriminate against those who have criminal records, who bathe infrequently, who use vulgar speech and have improper social graces. Most of us choose mates within our own race, ethnic group, or religion, hence discriminating against mates who, save for those characteristics, might be just as suitable. According to the 1992 census, only 2.2 percent of Americans were married to someone outside their own race.[3] There is also evidence of discrimination based on physical attributes in politics: not many short men have been elected president of the United States. In fact, twenty-two out of forty-two presidents have been five feet, eleven inches and taller, well above the population's average height.[4] That is not an outcome that would be expected if height had nothing to do with choices.

Furthermore, discrimination is not consistent. Sometimes people discriminate against theater entertainment in favor of parties or against women in favor of men; and at other times and circumstances the same people do the opposite.

One might be tempted to argue that racial discrimination in marriage is trivial and does not have important social consequences requiring a legal or political remedy, as do other forms of racial discrimination. But it does have important social consequences. When there is assortive (non-random) mate selection, it heightens whatever group differences there are in the population.[5] When high-IQ people marry other high-IQ people, when high-income people marry other high-income people, and to the extent there is a racial correlation between these characteristics, racial discrimination in mate selection enhances the inequality in the population's intelligence and income distribution. There would be greater income equality if high-IQ and high-income people mated with their low-IQ and low-income counterparts. But I imagine that most of us would be horrified by the suggestion of a mandate to require such mating.[6]

It would appear that the term discrimination, defined simply as the act of choice, is morally neutral in the sense that there are no unambiguous standards that permit us to argue that the choice to attend the University of Chicago or to purchase a Bordeaux wine is more righteous than the choice to attend Harvard University and purchase a Burgundy wine. More important, no argument can be made for government forcing a person to select one university or wine over another. And none can be produced to force people to grant equal opportunity when choosing universities, wines, and marriage partners.

If people are free to discriminate in favor of, or against, a university or wine, what argument can be made against their having that same right with respect to choosing based on the race or sex characteristics of their mates, employees, tenants, or club members? If one shares the value of freedom of association, why should some associations be permitted and others denied? If a man is not permitted to bring a court action against a woman who refuses to deal with him, in the form of a dating or marital relationship or for any arbitrary reason she chooses, what is the case for bringing court action for other refusals to "deal," such as in employment, renting or selling a house, or club memberships?

Nobel Laureate Kenneth Arrow argues that "There are many varieties of liberalism, which draw the boundaries between social and individual action in different places, but all agree in rejecting racial discrimination, by which is meant allowing racial identification to have a place in an individual's life chances."[7] If "allowing racial identification to have a place in an individual's life chances" means refusal to deal, what policy recommendations emerge? Refusal to deal can apply to any setting, including activities like marriage, friendship, invitations to social gatherings and golf games, all of which might affect one's "life chances." If refusal to deal is permitted in one activity, for any arbitrary reason, what case can be made for not permitting it in others? The practical answer to this question has more to do with the threat of government violence against people who refuse to deal in prohibited ways than with any kind of internally consistent logic.

Prejudice

In much of the racial literature, prejudice is usually seen as suspicion, intolerance, or an irrational hatred of other races. Sometimes it is seen as oppression, as suggested by law Professor Khiara M. Bridges, when he says, "Therefore, if racial prejudice, the subordination of people of color, and White supremacy persist, they do so largely because the legal system sanctions them."[8] Other times, prejudice is understood to mean racial preferences as implied by Justice Sandra Day O'Connor, when she wrote for the majority in *Adarand Contractors, Inc. v. Pena* (1995), striking down a government set-aside: "[B]ecause that perception *especially when fostered by the Congress of the United States* can only exacerbate rather than reduce racial prejudice, it will delay the time when race will become a truly irrelevant, or at least insignificant, factor."[9]

These visions of prejudice expose analysts to the pitfalls of making ambiguous statements and advancing faulty arguments. A useful operational definition of prejudice can be found by examining its Latin root— *praejudicium,* meaning "to judge before the facts are known." Thus, we might define prejudicial acts as decision-making on the basis of incomplete information.

That kind of decision-making, before facts are known, is necessary and to be expected in a world of scarcity, uncertainty, complexity, costly information—and often erroneous interpretation of that information. Furthermore, different individuals might arrive at different interpretations even if confronted with the same information. Also, different people reach different decisions on just what constitutes the optimal quantity of information to gather prior to making decisions.

Consider a simple, yet intuitively appealing, example of how decisions might be made on the basis of incomplete information (and possibly erroneous interpretation of evidence). Suppose a fully grown tiger suddenly appeared in a room. A reliable prediction is that most individuals would endeavor to leave the room with great dispatch. Such a response to the tiger's presence is not likely to be based on any detailed information about the behavioral characteristics of that particular tiger. The response is more likely to be based upon one's stock of information about tigers as a class, through folklore and observations of other tigers. The individual prejudges the tiger; we might say he employs stereotypes. He simply ascribes known or surmised group characteristics to the individual tiger. He is not likely to seek additional information, because he calculates that the expected cost of acquiring an additional unit of information about that tiger, such as talking to or petting it, is likely to exceed the expected benefit. People seldom undertake an activity when they surmise that its expected cost will exceed its expected benefit.

Sometimes when people use the terms prejudice and stereotype, they are used pejoratively to refer to those whose chosen quantity of information for decision-making the observer deems too small. However, what constitutes the optimal quantity of information collected before decisions are made is subjectively determined by the individual's calculation of his own costs and benefits.

Information is not costless. To acquire an additional unit of it requires a sacrifice of time, effort, or other resources. People therefore seek to economize on information cost. In doing so, they tend to substitute less expensive forms of information for more expensive forms. Physical attributes are "cheap" to observe. If a particular physical attribute is perceived as correlated with a more costly-to-observe one, the observer might use that attribute as an estimator or proxy for the costly-to-observe attribute. The cheaply observed fact that an individual is short, an amputee, a black, or a woman provides what some people deem to be sufficient information for decision-making or predicting the presence of some other more costly-to-observe attribute. For example, if asked to identify individuals with doctorate degrees in physics only by observing race and sex, most of us would assign a higher probability that white or Asian males would have such degrees than black males or women. Such behavior is what decision theory expects: an unobservable attribute must be estimated from an observable one.

Stereotyping and prejudging can be independent of preferences. Observing a person's decision-making behavior does not allow us to say anything unambiguous about that person's personal preferences with regard to race, sex, ethnicity, and nationality.

A simple example can demonstrate this. Imagine the reader is on a particular university campus. He is asked to pick a five-person basketball team from a group of twenty students; if the team he selects wins the game, he wins $10,000. The group from which he is to choose consists of five black males, five white males, five black females, and five white females.

He has zero information about their basketball proficiency, and they appear otherwise indistinguishable except by race and sex. That is, they are identical in terms of other physical characteristics, such as weight and height. Assuming that the person's objective is to maximize his chances of winning, his selection would probably be dominated by black males. That choice would reflect the real-world associations he has seen between basketball proficiency and race and sex.

What can an observer, watching that person's choices, say about his race or sex preferences? Absolutely nothing unambiguous simply by observing choices based on race and sex. Moreover, a person bearing antipathy toward blacks would select in the identical fashion as everyone else—if maximizing winnings dominated his objectives. Furthermore, given the high correlation between race, sex, and basketball proficiency, would anyone care if the selector indulged a racial preference for white males or women? He would personally bear the cost of preference indulgence.

A vast number of decisions must be made during our lives. Some of them, such as deciding whether to greet a passerby in the morning, require relatively small amounts of information. Others, such as selecting a marriage partner, require large amounts. A person is not "prejudiced" or "unprejudiced." Rather, he always exhibits prejudiced behavior to the extent that he substitutes general information (prejudgment or stereotypes) that is less costly in exchange for specific information that's more costly. What distinguishes one person from another are their comparative degrees of prejudiced behavior when facing similar situations. For any given decision, some people will search for more information than will others.

Prejudging People

Physical characteristics can be used as proxies for other costly-to-observe characteristics. Some racial and ethnic groups have higher incidences of and mortality from various diseases than the national average. In 1998, rates of death from cardiovascular diseases were about 30 percent higher among black adults than among white adults. Cervical cancer rates were five times higher among Vietnamese women in the United States than among white women there. Pima Indians of Arizona have the highest-known diabetes rates in the world.[10] Prostate cancer is nearly twice as common among black men as white men.[11]

Approximately 80,000 Americans have sickle-cell disease. About 9 percent of blacks have the trait. One in every 1,000 to 1,400 American Hispanic children is born with sickle-cell disease itself. The high incidence of the sickle-cell gene in these and other specific populations is due to their ability to make red blood cells resistant to the malaria parasite.

Whether genetics, environment, or other factors account for the association between race and some diseases, it is undeniable that such an association exists. Thus, a physical characteristic such as race can be used as an indicator of the higher probability of some other characteristic, such as prostate cancer and cervical cancer. Health-care providers can therefore better assess patient screening needs; for example, they can prescribe more frequent blood tests for the prostate-specific antigen (the well-known PSA test) for black males. They can employ what is derisively called racial profiling. One might take the position that while it is legitimate for doctors to use race or ethnicity as indicators of the higher probability of certain diseases, it is not legitimate to use those two characteristics as indicators for worker productivity, criminal behavior, or basketball proficiency. Other than simply stating that it is acceptable to use race or ethnicity as a predictor in medicine but not in other areas of life, is there really a difference? Surely race and ethnicity are not perfect indicators of the risk of prostate cancer or hypertension; neither are they perfect indicators of SAT scores, criminal behavior, or basketball/football/sprinting skill.

However, there *are* concrete factual data that indicate such associations. For example: In 2002, the average black score on the combined math and verbal portions of the SAT was 857, the average white score 23 percent higher—at 1060.[12] While blacks are 13 percent of the population, they constitute 80 percent of professional basketball players and 65 percent of professional football players. Blacks who trace their ancestry to West Africa, including black Americans, have achieved more than 95 percent of the best times in sprinting.[13] For the crime of homicide, over the years 1976–2000, blacks, while 13 percent of the general population, made up 51.5 percent of the offenders; whites were 46.4 percent, and others 2 percent.[14]

Racial Profiling

Using race as an indicator does not necessarily tell us anything about the chooser's racial preferences. The Washington Lawyers Committee filed a lawsuit in April 2001 on behalf of Bryan Greene, a black man, against Your Way Taxicab Company for violations of 42 U.S.C. sec. 1981 and the District of Columbia's Human Rights Act, both of which prohibit discrimination in the making of contracts. As Greene approached a hotel entrance, the doorman was assisting a customer out of a Your Way Taxicab. The doorman saw Greene and attempted to hold the cab for him; however, when the driver spotted Greene, he sped away. After mediation, Your Way Taxicab Company reached an out-of-court settlement.[15]

In a number of cities, there have been complaints by blacks of similar behavior by cab drivers. The question we might ask is this: are the drivers' decisions based on racial preferences, or might they fear being asked to go into a neighborhood where there is a high probability of being robbed, assaulted, or murdered? By simply knowing that a driver refused a black passenger, we cannot make an unambiguous statement about whether the decision was motivated by racial preferences.

Evidence that the taxi driver's decisions might very well be based on criteria other than racial preferences is seen in a 1999 story written by James Owens, titled "Capital Cabbies Salute Race Profiling." Owens said:

> If racial profiling is "racism," then the cab drivers of Washington, D.C., they themselves mainly blacks and Hispanics, are all for it. A District taxi-cab commissioner, Sandra Seegars, who is black, issued a safety-advice statement urging D.C.'s 6,800 cabbies to refuse to pick up "dangerous looking" passengers. She described "dangerous looking" as a "young black guy ... with shirttail hanging down longer than his coat, baggy pants, unlaced tennis shoes," etc. That's one typical description—but the cabbies know, from fear-filled experience, about many other "looks" of black-male threat, especially at night. She also warned cabbies to stay away from low-income black neighborhoods (which comprise much of Washington, D.C.). Her action was triggered by the most recent murder of a cabbie in Southeast Washington.[16]

Another example of race as an indicator stems from a case in which residents in Southwest Washington filed suit in a U.S. district court after Domino's Pizza repeatedly refused to make home deliveries in certain neighborhoods and instead made customers meet drivers at curbside to pay for and receive their orders. The lawsuit alleged racial discrimination by Domino's Pizza and Team Washington, a company that operates more than 50 Domino's stores. According to the plaintiffs, Domino's delivers to the door in Georgetown and other mostly white areas of Northwest Washington. The suit also alleged that deliverymen engaged in similar delivery decisions in Southeast Washington's Potomac Gardens, where another customer filed a bias lawsuit. Again, the question is whether the drivers were acting on the basis of racial preference or out of fear of assault or robbery?

According to *Pizza Marketing Quarterly,* similar charges of racial discrimination were filed in St. Louis against Papa John's pizza delivery. Cathy Juengel, a St. Louis Papa John's district manager, said she could not and would not ask her drivers to put their lives on the line. She added that the racial discrimination accusation was false, because 75 to 85 percent of the drivers servicing the complaining neighborhood were black and, moreover, most of those drivers lived in the very neighborhood being denied full delivery service.[17] One doubts that black pizza deliverers can be charged with disliking black people.

The Reverend Jesse Jackson once said, "There is nothing more painful for me at this stage in my life than to walk down the street and hear footsteps and start thinking about robbery—then look around and see somebody white and feel relieved."[18] A former Los Angeles police chief, Bernard Parks, defending racial profiling, said, "It's not the fault of the police when they stop minority males or put them in jail. It's the fault of the minority males for committing the crime. In my mind it is not a great revelation that if officers are looking for criminal activity, they're going to look at the kind of people who are listed on crime reports."[19] Charleston, South Carolina, Chief of Police Reuben Greenberg argued that the problem facing black America is not racial profiling. He said, "the greatest problem in the black community is the tolerance for high levels of criminality."

The percentages of black arrests for selected crimes, found in *Crime in the United States, 2006: Uniform Crime Reports,* bear out the disproportionate criminal activity by blacks: murder and non-negligent manslaughter (51 percent), robbery (56 percent), aggravated assault (35 percent), and vehicle theft (34 percent). For blacks under the age of 18, the percentages are even more startling: murder and non-negligent manslaughter (60), robbery (67), aggravated assault (42), and vehicle theft (43).[20] Although racial profiling is often seen as racism, I doubt that anyone could find much evidence for a claim that Jesse Jackson, black police chiefs Bernard Parks and Reuben Greenberg, black taxi drivers, and black pizza deliverers are racists.

The law-abiding black citizen who is passed up by a taxi, refused pizza delivery, or stopped by the police can rightfully feel a sense of injustice and resentment. But the bulk of those feelings should be directed at those who have made race synonymous with higher rates of criminal activity rather than the taxi driver or pizza deliverer who is trying to earn a living and avoid being a crime victim.

Racial Preferences

People have likes and dislikes for many things. In everyday language, as well as in economic analysis, an individual is said to prefer object A to object B if, being free to choose, he chooses A rather than B. There are no objective criteria by which we can judge whether one set of preferences is better or more righteous than another. There are no commonly accepted standards to prove, for example, that it is better for a person to prefer Bordeaux wines to those of Burgundy or to prefer three-piece suits to blue jeans. For a person to say that a preference for Bordeaux over Burgundy is sensible or more righteous is plain nonsense. To conclude that he should be indifferent to the distinctions between them is also nonsense. To say that Bordeaux wine is better than Burgundy wine is simply a value judgment in a debate that can go on forever; it boils down to a matter of tastes and opinion.

The absence of standards for evaluating statements dealing with better and best is found in all sciences. For example, it is meaningless, and in fact nonsense, for a physicist to suggest or even entertain a discussion about whether a gaseous state is better than a liquid or solid state or whether they are equally good. So far as human choice is concerned, the most we can ever say objectively is whether, given a set of preferences and the constraints of prices and income, an individual is or is not doing the best he can.

The same holds true when it comes to individual preferences for human physical attributes, such as height, weight, a "richly" endowed body, and hair color: these are solely matters of individual taste. To the extent that individuals have preferences for or against human physical attributes in general, we also expect people to exhibit preferences for or against racial attributes. From an objective analytical point of view, there are no conceptual distinctions between racial preferences and preferences for other objects of desire.

It might be argued that racial preferences are not comparable to other kinds in terms of the consequences they have for society and for individuals. Although the indulgence of racial preferences has specific effects that the indulgence for, say, certain wines does not, are they basically different? If so, how? The preference for Bordeaux wines "harms" Burgundy producers by reducing the value of resources held in Burgundy production. If the consequences of preferences are generally thought to reduce the value of some resources and increase the value of others, then it can be said that preferences for physical attributes have effects similar to those of other preferences. The essential difference—by no means small—between preferences for racial features and those for wines is that the latter are not as specialized as the former. In other words, if Burgundy producers see that consumers prefer Bordeaux, they theoretically would be able to convert their resources into Bordeaux production. On the other hand, people who are black cannot become white.[21]

The fact that racial characteristics are specialized or unchangeable does not place them in a class by themselves. Persons with average IQs are generally preferred to those with below-average IQs, and persons who are not physically disabled are preferred to those who are. In each of these cases, and many others, the less-preferred physical attribute is unchangeable; and in each case, the less-preferred person suffers a disadvantage in some competitive arenas. This disadvantage is to be expected. Disadvantage and advantage are inevitable consequences of differences in individual tastes, abilities, and traits on the one hand, and freedom of choice in an open society on the other.

Human preferences—whether for such physical attributes as race, food, child-rearing practices, or entertainment—can have a moral dimension. There may be a moral consensus condemning preferences for forms of entertainment such as pornographic movies and a consensus that condemns indulgence of racial preferences. The fact of a consensus on what constitutes moral or immoral preferences does not alter the facts: people do exhibit preference; and there is no commonly agreed-upon standard for assessing which preferences are better than others. The best we can hope for, in terms of objective analysis, is to take human preferences as a given and then use economic theory to analyze how people choose in the face of objective constraints of price and income.

If there can be a moral dimension to preference indulgence, it should be to oblige people to pay for their preferences. Open markets make this possible, and as a result there is less tendency to indulge preferences. For example, at one time there were no black professional basketball and football players. Today, black players dominate both sports. That came about without anti-discrimination litigation and racial-employment preferences. It resulted from the natural actions of markets and competition among teams that could not ignore a huge pool of black talent.

Suppose a particular basketball or football team owner decides that he is going to indulge his racial preferences against black players by not hiring them. Many fans, both black and white, might find his actions reprehensible and attendance would fall. The team's winning record is likely to be lower. Plus, he would have to raise the salaries he was willing to pay in order to acquire highly productive white players. His racial-preference indulgence could cost him tens of millions of dollars in the forms of lost revenue and higher costs. So we would not expect a basketball or football team owner to indulge any preferences he might have against blacks.

While the basketball and football example is easy to visualize, the same forces are at work in other markets. If an employer chooses to discriminate against blacks, he will have to pay higher wages for white workers. The black person he shunned will be available to employers who might be more interested in profits than in indulging their racial preferences at wages less than the discriminating employer has to pay.

When analyzing racial phenomena, we must be careful to distinguish among the three determinants of choice: preference, prejudice, and real differences. If we assume that racial preferences are the root of the problem we are addressing—when prejudice or real differences are a better explanation—we will derive erroneous conclusions, and promote policy that is ineffectual and possibly harmful to its intended beneficiaries. Let us briefly examine several areas where racial preferences are generally assumed to be the villain.

Hiring and Employment Discrimination

Many recruitment and hiring practices are often said to reflect racial preferences, but an alternative explanation might be drawn from our previous discussion about seeking information. When a company sets out to hire workers, it must discover how productive those seeking jobs are and whether they are suitable for training. Since this process costs money, an employer has an incentive to select a recruitment strategy with a high probability of success. For example, if there is thought to be a correlation between the candidate's performance and the quality of the high school he attended, some recruitment costs can be reduced just by knowing that simple detail. Research by Professor Abigail Thernstrom found that:

> [I]n 1998, the average seventeen-year-old African American could only read as well as the typical white child who had not yet reached age thirteen. In 1992, just 18 percent of black students in twelfth grade were rated 'proficient' or 'advanced' in reading, as compared with 47 percent of whites. As of 1998, those numbers were unchanged. . . . The most recent data thus show black students in twelfth grade dealing with scientific problems at the level of whites in the sixth grade and writing about as well as whites in the eighth grade.[22] This poor primary and secondary school academic achievement is reflected in the performance of college-bound black seniors who took the Scholastic Aptitude Test (SAT). Nationally the combined average SAT for blacks in 2008 was 1276 out of a possible 2400; whites and Asians scored respectively 1581 and 1623.[23]

Given those statistics, race might be a fairly good, though not perfect, indicator of expected worker productivity. One should therefore not be surprised that employers take race into account when assessing worker productivity. To observe a process that selects in part by race and to attribute the selection to preferences (in this case, to employer "racism") may be misleading. One example of this misunderstanding occurs when researchers perform "paired testing" as a means to discover racial discrimination in employment, housing, or insurance. Paired testing matches individuals in terms of such qualifications as age, education, experience, credit record, and other factors deemed important to an employer, landlord, or insurance agent. They differ only by race or sex, and researchers get to see whether they are treated differently. Authors Michael Fix and Margery Turner say that "Paired testing is an excellent vehicle for understanding and measuring actual discrimination understood here simply as the practice of treating people differently because of their membership in a protected group."[24]

Objective qualifications are only part of the information an employer or landlord wants to know prior to making a decision about whether to employ or rent to an individual. An employer or landlord might deem other information—such as trustworthiness, promptness, congeniality, respect for property, and other personal attributes—an important part of the decision. Whether a person is white or black, objective qualifications do not adequately convey information about those attributes. Prior employment or rental references might not be reliable, because previous employers or renters might fear legal reprisals for giving candid references. Employers or landlords could hire private detectives to get such information, but might deem that too costly and therefore resort to cheaper methods: hunches, race or sex, word-of-mouth opinion, and existing references from employers.

There are demographic differences between races that increase the likelihood that race can be used as a proxy for more costly-to-observe attributes. To assume that because a white and a black both have a high school diploma or a bachelor's degree, they have equal levels of academic proficiency ignores reality. There are significant differences by race as seen in SAT scores for admittance to college and on tests such as GRE, LSAT, and MCAT that are used in admissions to graduate and professional schools. The racial gap in scores on these tests suggests that on the average a high school diploma or a BA degree held by a black is not the same as one held by a white. None of this is to say that every black with a high school diploma or a BA degree shares the group characteristics, but how does an employer know?

The auto insurance industry provides a nonracial example of the use of physical attributes, Drivers under twenty-five years of age are charged routinely higher premiums. But one doubts that auto insurance companies can be charged with disliking young people. Life insurance companies charge women lower premiums. Can we reasonably assert that life insurance companies like women and dislike men? In both cases, a physical attribute acts as a proxy for an unobservable attribute. In the case of driver age, there is a higher probability of accident claims and, in the case of the insured's sex, longer life expectancy.[25]

Suppose an employer has racially neutral preferences and is uncertain about average black worker productivity relative to whites. What would encourage or discourage him from seeking more information and experimenting with and perhaps revising his beliefs? Laws or practices that require him to pay all workers identical wages and laws that make it very costly to fire a worker reduce employer incentive to experiment. A nonracial example might be helpful.

Imagine that a new supermarket, unfamiliar to local customers, locates in an area of established markets. The latter have considerable customer loyalty. How can the new arrival induce customers to try it out? The method typically employed is to offer sales, perhaps also prizes, coupons, and other amenities, all of which are effective means of attracting customers.

Just as easily, customers can be given an inducement not to experiment. Imagine there was legislation requiring that all supermarkets charge identical prices and sell their goods on identical terms. That being the case, one cannot think of much inducement for customers, who already have loyalty to established supermarkets, to experiment with the newcomer. Imagine there was also a law stipulating that once a customer chose a market, he had to stick with it or go through very costly procedures to change. In other words, if he was dissatisfied with the supermarket, he could not cheaply "fire" it by taking his business elsewhere. It is very easy to predict the response of customers to the new supermarket: why experiment and incur the risk?

Continuing with this scenario, one should not be surprised if incumbent supermarket owners invested in lobbying for the creation of a law mandating sales on identical terms. It would be to their financial advantage to reduce customer incentive to experiment by making experimentation more costly. Moreover, political justification for the promotion of these laws could be couched in glowing, civic-minded terms like the prevention of cutthroat competition and encouraging level playing fields.

In some respects, this example can be applied to labor markets. Labor laws or collective bargaining agreements that mandate equal starting wages reduce employer incentives to experiment. Similarly, anti-discrimination regulations make experimentation costly. Once a black employee is hired, it may be very expensive to fire him if the employer deems he has made a mistake. The employee's lawyer could tie up much of the company's resources in litigation. Whatever increases the cost of firing an employee also has the effect of increasing the cost to hire.

Home Mortgage Discrimination

A study of mortgage-bank lending practices reported that black and Hispanic applicants were denied credit in greater proportions than white, even when income was comparable. Moreover, the study reported similar disparities in application denials among neighborhoods classified by race and income.[26] A staff writer for the *The Wall Street Journal* interpreted the report as follows: "[I]f you're black, it's twice as likely your mortgage application will be rejected as it is if you're white. And if you live in a low-income neighborhood, chances are that many lenders have little interest in mortgage-lending in your community anyway."[27] Referring to the study, economist Julianne Malveaux wrote that blacks continue to be segregated "because of well-documented discrimination in mortgage lending."[28] Jesse Jackson said it is criminal that banks "systematically discriminate against African-Americans and Latinos in making mortgage loans."[29]

While rejections of loan applications differ significantly between the groups discussed above, we cannot unambiguously assign the difference to racial preferences; there might be some *real* differences. The Home Mortgage Disclosure Act data used by the study has serious limitations. It does not contain information about applicant assets and creditworthiness. An important element in assessing the creditworthiness of individuals is their net worth. Defined as the difference between the value of assets and debts owed, net worth differs significantly between blacks and whites. As of 1984, white households had a median net worth of $39,140, while that for black households was $3,400.

Net-worth differences between blacks and whites vary a great deal regardless of income. In the $2,000 to $3,999 monthly income category, a white household's net worth was $50,529; for blacks, $15,977. In the

$4,000 income per month and more, white net worth was $128,237, and for blacks, it was $58,758.[30] In 2000, white households had a median net worth of $79,400, black households $7,500.[31] In the third (middle) income quintile, white net worth was $59,500, while that for blacks was $11,500. In the fifth (highest) income quintile, white net worth was $208, 023, and for blacks it was $65,141.[32]

Given the history of blacks in the United States, it should not be surprising that they have not accumulated, through work or inheritance, as many assets as have whites. But that fact in no way implies racial discrimination by banks as an explanation for racial differences in loan approval rates. Since net worth is one of the determinants of creditworthiness, it suggests that blacks as a group will qualify for fewer loans, even in a society with neutral racial preferences.

Racial preferences as an explanation for the higher incidence of loan denial to blacks and Hispanics loses some of its appeal when we examine the data further. The following are the loan denials by percent for conventional loans, according to a 1992 *Federal Reserve Bulletin:* blacks (38), American Indian (27), Hispanics (27), whites (17), and Asians (15).[33] Ignored in the debate over the mortgage application-approval gap between whites and blacks is whether white-owned mortgage banks *also* discriminate against whites, since the banks approved a greater percentage of mortgage applications of Asian-Americans than whites. No doubt the explanation is not racial preferences against whites at all. Japanese and Chinese-Americans are on the average financially more successful and have better credit ratings than do whites on average. When Alicia Munnell, author of the Federal Reserve study, was interviewed by two *Forbes* reporters, she conceded that the report did not sufficiently take into account differences in creditworthiness, adding: "I do not have evidence ... [n]o one has evidence" of lending bias.[34]

Another factor to consider is that if banks maintained a policy of stiffer loan approval requirements for blacks, the default rates among blacks would be lower than those for whites. The Federal Reserve study found that black and white default rates are roughly equivalent.

In 1999, Freddie Mac, the huge mortgage lender, conducted a consumer credit survey. In addition, Freddie Mac and the historically black colleges and universities convened more than fifty focus groups. The survey found that nearly twice as many blacks as whites have bad credit. Specifically, 47 percent of blacks and 34 percent of Hispanics had bad credit, compared to 27 percent of whites. Among people with incomes under $25,000, the figures were 48 percent for blacks and 31 percent for whites; among higher income-earners ($65,000 to $75,000), 34 percent for blacks and 20 percent for whites.[35]

Racial discrimination as an explanation for differences in loan rejections loses more credibility when assessed by the findings of a 2002 study, "A Test of Cultural Affinity in Home Mortgage Lending," conducted by Raphael W. Bostic, former economist at the Federal Reserve Board in Washington.[36] Professor Bostic surveyed forty minority-owned and 106 white-owned banks. He found that, in 1995, minority-owned banks rejected black loan applicants at a rate double that of their white-owned counterparts: 35 percent of black loan applications were denied at minority-owned banks and 17 percent at white-owned banks. The denial rate for Latino applicants at minority-owned banks was 16 percent versus 13 percent, respectively. In the case of Asian loan applicants, bank ownership had little or no effect on denial rates. (Black-owned banks historically have invested a greater percentage of their loan portfolio *outside* the community in which they are located.)[37]

Subprime Mortgage Problem

Between 1994 and 2003, overall home ownership grew from 64 to 68 percent of the population, as the residents of 9 million more households became homeowners. The greatest gains in home ownership occurred among blacks (1.2 million) and Hispanics (1.9 million). Nearly one-half of black and Hispanic households are homeowners compared to the white rate of 71 percent.[38]

A major stimulus to minority home ownership has been increased access to credit through the 1980 Depository Institutions Deregulatory and Monetary Control Act's elimination of usury controls on first-lien mortgage rates and the 1990s' strengthening of the provisions of the Community Reinvestment Act of 1977; the latter is a federal law that requires banks to offer credit throughout their entire market and discourages them from restricting their credit services to high-income areas. The Federal Housing Administration, which guarantees mortgage loans, liberalized its rules for guaranteeing mortgages. These and other factors combined to give lenders financial inducement to make mortgage loans to those who posed an elevated credit risk and had weak credit histories. In contrast to the past, instead of a lender denying riskier applicants a mortgage, he made the loan at a higher interest rate.

Blacks and Hispanics pose higher credit risks. Thus, one should not be surprised to see them disproportionately represented among subprime borrowers. Blacks make up 27 percent of the number of subprime home-purchase loans, and 21 percent of subprime home-equity loans, while Hispanics, respectively, make up 20 and 15 percent; those figures compare to whites, who respectively make up 7 and 6 percent. As of 2003, the foreclosure status and serious delinquency on prime loans were, respectively, .48 and 1.1 percent; those for subprime loans, 3.4 and 7.4.[39]

According to an article in the *Atlanta Journal-Constitution,* "Black Atlantans often snared by subprime loans," a national study of credit scores—not just mortgage loan applicants—found that 52 percent of blacks have scores that would classify them as subprime borrowers compared with 16 percent of whites.[40] Such a finding contradicts the suggestion of racial discrimination in a *New York Times* editorial, which said that "blacks and Hispanic borrowers were far more likely to be steered into high-cost subprime loans than other borrowers, even after controlling for factors such as income, loan size and property location."[41]

Prior to the emergence of the subprime market for home mortgages, lending institutions rationed credit by denying risky loans and those involving some property locations, a practice that became known as redlining and was attacked as racial discrimination. Interestingly, now that legal ceilings on home mortgage interests have been relaxed, enabling less creditworthy people to secure loans, the racial discrimination charges focus on higher loan-default rates experienced by people who would have otherwise not been able to secure a loan.

Public policy directed at mortgage-lender racial discrimination will miss its mark and may, like affirmative action in lending, possibly exacerbate the credit problems of blacks. Banks will simply move away. A more effective policy would attempt to reduce the high cost and risks of lending in inner-city neighborhoods. When what is prejudice (as we have defined it) and response to real differences are misdiagnosed as racial preferences, misguided policy will emerge.

Discrimination against Low-Income Shoppers

During the mid-1960s, it was widely alleged that white merchants in ghetto areas exploited their customers by charging higher prices and selling lower-quality merchandise. The merchants, it was said, were seeking to earn above-normal profits as a way of acting out their racial hostility toward blacks.[42] But it turns out that racial hostility by merchants could not adequately explain the higher prices.

They were indeed higher in black neighborhoods, and several studies showed that retail food chains followed different pricing policies between them and white neighborhoods. With these findings in hand, the Federal Trade Commission (FTC), along with consumer advocacy groups and public-interest lawyers, attempted through public pressure to oblige merchants to offer black and white customers the same terms.

To view the merchants' behavior as exploitative or racist ignores the fact that black neighborhoods tend to be high-cost business environments. Losses from business-related crime are higher there than elsewhere as a percentage of total sales; business, fire, and theft insurance premiums are also higher; and it is riskier to extend credit. In addition, because of the low income of many black residents and the effect of that on sales mix and volume, merchandising techniques used to lower sales costs in higher-income neighborhoods are not as readily adaptable to low-income areas.

High crime rates figure in another, unappreciated way. One of the goals of a supermarket manager is to maximize the rate of merchandise turnover per square foot of leased or owned space. When theft is relatively low, the supermarket can make use of space along the exit aisles and entryways. Often merchandise such as plants, fertilizer, and other home and garden items is placed outside of the store and sometimes left overnight. Therefore, a merchant can use all of the space he pays for, which raises his profit potential. That merchandising technique is unavailable in localities where there is less overall honesty. Merchandise cannot be located near exits and out of sight of store employees. If it is placed outside, the merchant must bear the expense of having it guarded, and leaving it out overnight is out of the question. Unlike low-crime neighborhoods, the merchant must pay for square footage he cannot use, thus lowering his profit potential. In addition, it is not unusual to see uniformed guards on duty at supermarkets in high-crime areas.

Much of the behavior that critics have condemned is therefore merely an economic response to an environment that has a higher cost of doing business. If products and services are to be provided in higher-cost neighborhoods, prices must reflect that cost. Evidence substantiates this explanation of merchant behavior. The FTC has shown that while gross margins were higher in black neighborhoods, the difference was more than accounted for by higher operating costs and a lower return on equity.[43] The assertion that above-normal profits were earned becomes even less credible when we recognize that retailing is characterized by relative ease of entry, so that if above-normal profits existed, one would expect to see merchants opening new businesses until profits in black and white neighborhood areas were equal. The opposite of this has occurred in urban areas: businesses have left without being replaced.

The crusade that blamed the problem of the black consumer on the greed and racism of whites may well have had a negative impact on consumer welfare. The adverse publicity and boycotts (and other actions) against merchants in black communities gave merchants increased incentive to move out. The result is fewer neighborhood stores, with shoppers being forced to travel longer distances or pay even higher local prices than in the past.

High crime takes a toll on consumers in another way. In low-crime neighborhoods, FedEx, UPS, and other delivery companies often leave merchandise at the door if no one answers. In high-crime neighborhoods, that is not an option. The companies must bear the costs of making return trips, or the customer has to bear the cost of traveling to pick up his goods.

Conclusions

In today's America, there is a broad consensus that race-based discrimination in many activities is morally offensive and in many cases rightfully illegal—as it should be when there is taxpayer-based provision of such goods and services as public schools and universities, libraries, and social services. Even though people should be free to deal with, or refuse to deal with, anyone in private matters, there is little evidence that race-based discrimination is widespread in today's America. After all, there is a difference between what people can do and what they find it in their interest to do. That conclusion is suggested by laws that once codified racial discrimination in the United States and elsewhere. In this country, there were antimiscegenation laws and restrictive covenants. During South Africa's apartheid era, there were also job-reservation statutes and others that reserved amenities such as theaters, restaurants, and hotels for whites only.

One of the first implications of the existence of a law is that not everyone will voluntarily behave according to its specifications. Otherwise, there would be no need for the law. After all, to the writer's knowledge, there is no legal requirement that people eat or avoid tossing their weekly earnings onto the street. Yet we need not worry because most people will not find it in their private interest to do either.

CHAPTER 7

Summary and Conclusion

Primum non nocere
—Hippocratic Oath

THE UNDERLYING PREMISE of this book is that racial discriminatory preferences do not explain all they are purported to explain. This is not to say that racial discrimination does not exist and has no effects. The policy-relevant question is how much of what we see can be explained by discrimination alone and how much by other phenomena?

Elementary economic theory amply demonstrates there are differences between what people would *like* to do, what they *can* do, and what they will find in their interest to do. Simply the knowledge that a person prefers Rolls-Royces to Fords, or twenty-five-point diamonds to two-point diamonds, does not tell us much about what he will in fact purchase. To understand more fully what people will do, one must also know the restraints they face and what must be sacrificed. In other words, we must acknowledge the role income and prices play in human behavior.

Differences between what people want to do and what they can do, or find it in their self-interest to do, apply to matters of race as well. Efforts to form discriminatory collusions against blacks encounter problems akin to efforts to form other kinds of collusive agreements. The major problem is that what is optimal for an individual member most likely will not be optimal for the group as a whole. For example, when a seller's collusion is organized, it pays an individual member to cheat by charging a lower price while other members honor the one agreed upon. By shading their prices, the members who cheat can sell more of their product and earn greater profits at the expense of faithful members.

There is symmetry in buyer collusions. It pays an individual member to offer a higher price while other members honor the agreement to offer the lower one. Because of differences between what is optimal for the individual and what is optimal for the group, voluntary collusions (those not legally enforced) tend to break down.

A racial example of the difficulty of maintaining an effective collusion is the post-Civil War attempts by Southern planters—buyers of labor—to depress wages for blacks. During the Reconstruction era, many landowners resented the mobility and increased bargaining power of freedmen. Landowners therefore often colluded in an attempt to restrict the terms of sharecropping contracts. Before the Joint Committee on Reconstruction, in 1866, General George E. Spencer told of a planters' association in Tuscaloosa County, Alabama. The planters agreed among themselves to give no more than one-eighth of the net proceeds of their crops to black tenants. One landowner violated the agreement and contracted to give his tenants one-sixth. He was later ostracized and forced to change the contract.

Newspapers and journals of the time carried numerous appeals for landowner cooperation and organization. In 1865, a contributor to the *Southern Cultivator* urged that planters stand together in enforcing contracts; with landlords acting as one, the freedman "must consent or starve." Four years later, in *DeBow's Review,* a planter lamented that "there is no concert of action on the part of the planters to oppose these ever increasing exactions [wage demands of the freedmen]." The same lament was aired in the same magazine in 1889: "If they desire success, let the farmers, as a body, cooperate together, and work by rule, order and system; attend to their own labor, and let other's labor alone."[1] This latter plea was in response to one white farmer, motivated by high demand for agricultural products and subsequent high demand for agricultural labor, "enticing" another's workers by offering higher wages.

An official of the Freedmen's Bureau correctly saw why planter collusions failed: "Such was the demand for negro laborers . . . that any combination to abridge their freedom in seeking and changing homes, or to control the price of labor, failed utterly."[2] General Wager Swayne said,

"[T]he planters made a strong combination to hire no negro away from home. The freedmen stood it out until the planters gave way, and they finally hired at random, at a little higher wages than were generally paid elsewhere."[3] Another general referred to "a competition for labor which in many localities [in Texas], has become a scramble."[4]

Planters' associations failed to organize an effective collusion against black labor. That is precisely what economic theory would predict: the goals of a collusion and actually achieving those goals are often two different things. The reason for the planters' failure is simple: profits depended on getting crops planted, harvested, and off to the market. Planters willing to pay higher wages found more workers willing to work for them; in addition, they could pick and choose among workers to get those of higher quality, while planters who honored the lower-wage agreement found fewer and lower-quality workers. Strong individual incentives to violate agreements, plus the absence of an enforcement technique, were the Achilles heel of the planter collusion.

As sellers of labor, trade unions are collusions. Like buyer collusions, they encounter similar problems. It is in a union's interest to set high wages for its members. However, not all workers in a given occupation are — or are allowed to become — union members. Although a union can set wages for its members, it cannot do so for non-members. As we saw in our discussion of the railroad industry, in the pursuit of higher profits, employers were only too anxious to hire the cheaper-priced black workers who were denied union membership. Unions of course learned in the construction, trucking, plumbing, and other industries that what could not be successfully accomplished through the free market could be accomplished through violence — and later through government backing in the form of restrictive labor laws and regulations, such as occupational licensure and the Davis-Bacon, Interstate Commerce, and National Labor Relations acts. Those measures put the force of government behind collusive agreements.

Another example of racially discriminatory collusions breaking down can be found in major league baseball and professional football. In baseball, the large pool of talented players in the Negro leagues, and the fact that such talent could not be ignored and denied indefinitely, made it only a matter of time before racial collusion in professional sports would break down. In 1947, when the Brooklyn Dodgers signed Jackie Robinson to a contract, and two years later hired two other black players, the rest of the league teams decided they could not continue to suffer the competitive disadvantage from discriminating against the large pool of available, highly qualified blacks.

Today, black athletes dominate areas of sports where they were once excluded. As of 1985, over 75 percent of American professional basketball players, 54 percent of professional football players, and 20 percent of professional baseball players were black.[5] In professional basketball, twenty-one of the twenty-six times the Most Valuable Player award was won, between 1955 and 1981, it was won by a black.[6] Black players tend to be the highest paid. As early as 1970, four of the six baseball players in the $125,000 and higher salary bracket were black.[7] As the twenty-first century begins, blacks dominate professional sports, with the exception of baseball, even more so.

There have been many successful collusions, and they have worked against the best interests of blacks. The reason is simply that the conditions for their breakdown have not been present. Effective collusions require an enforcement mechanism that may include, *inter alia*, the following: penalties for noncompliance with the terms of the collusion, state-enforced laws or standards, and noncomplying members denied the right to do business; and licenses or special privileges revoked for "unethical" behavior."[8] The ultimate enforcement mechanism is threat of violence, usually at the hands of government. When there is government enforcement of collusive action, paying a higher price or charging a lower price becomes more than a matter of failing to honor a gentlemen's agreement; it becomes a criminal act subject to fines and/or imprisonment.

When there are government-sanctioned collusions, as in the cases of the minimum wage law, the Davis-Bacon Act, collective bargaining agreements established under the Railway Labor and Wagner acts, and numerous licensing arrangements, employers achieve lower costs by engaging in racially discriminatory hiring. There is less economic inducement for employers to take advantage of lower wages and hire less-preferred workers and risk racial conflict in the workplace. Whatever the moral and emotional arguments over whether it is fair for one person to have to charge a lower price for what he sells or pay a higher price for what he buys, the effects of preventing him from doing so are clear: the competitive disadvantages he already faces are heightened. After all, the most effective way to get somebody to buy something or hire someone is to offer a lower price or wage.

Further appreciation of the ability of competitive forces to thwart those of racial discrimination is seen in housing markets by considering this question: how did blacks seize control of housing in the central areas of most major cities? During the more racially discriminatory times of the 1930s, '40s, and '50s, no one could prevent whole blocks and neighborhoods from going from white to black virtually overnight. How did poor, discriminated-against blacks do this? Keep in mind that some of these neighborhoods were formerly occupied by relatively affluent whites. Moreover, there were no anti-discriminatory housing laws and no fair-housing advocates, such as the federal Department of Housing and Urban Development.

Poor blacks simply outbid the whites for the property. At first thought, the ability of poor people to outbid those of greater means may seem implausible. But imagine a three-story brownstone being rented by a non-poor white family for $200 per month. Imagine, too, that the landlord has antipathy toward blacks. Despite his antipathy, if six poor black families proposed that the building be partitioned into six units, with them paying a rent of $75 per unit, the landlord might very well reassess his position. He would be faced with the prospect of earning $450 a month by renting to blacks as opposed to $200 a month by indulging his racial preferences and retaining his white tenant. The fact that blacks came to occupy neighborhoods formerly occupied by whites is strong evidence that the landlord's dilemma was resolved in favor of blacks.

That example demonstrates how price-fixing and other restrictions on trade can reduce options for people who are discriminated against. If there were a rent-control law, mandating that the maximum rental income the landlord could charge was $200 a month, less-preferred renters could not compete with those more preferred. That in turn means a transaction deemed mutually beneficial (the one between the six black families and the landlord) would not have occurred.

Why is it that poor blacks did not inundate suburban areas to the extent they did the cities? The answer is easy: the power of local governments to subvert the operation of the market. To a much greater extent than cities, suburban areas have highly restrictive zoning ordinances. They fix the minimum lot size, set minimum floor space and minimum distance to adjacent houses, and restrict property use to a single family. These laws combined, independent of de jure or de facto racial discrimination, deny poor people the chance to compete with *non*poor people.

Therein lies the power of the market. People can offset some of their handicaps by offering a higher price for what they buy or a lower price for what they sell—what economists call compensating differences. Well-meaning observers may be morally outraged by such a necessity. But the fact of business is that if less-preferred people are not permitted to use price as a bargaining tool, they may very well end up with none of what they want instead of some of it.[9]

As we have discussed throughout, numerous laws, regulations, and ordinances have reduced or eliminated avenues of upward mobility for many blacks. The most common feature of these barriers is that they prevent people from making voluntary transactions that are deemed mutually advantageous by the transactors themselves. While there is a long history of licensing laws written with the express purpose of restricting opportunities for blacks, it is misleading to see those laws as necessarily *anti*-black. An ordinance that generates a $600,000 license price in order to own a taxi, such as in New York City, discriminates against and handicaps *anyone*—brown, black, white, or yellow—who cannot meet the price. Therefore, these laws are anti-people! They produce a racial effect only to the extent that blacks may be the least likely to meet the entry conditions. They were the last major ethnic group to become urbanized and gain basic civil rights. When they finally achieved that status, blacks found that new barriers had been erected.

Recognizing that laws creating economic barriers are anti-people is important, not for analytical clarity alone but for making policy recommendations as well. For example, people who financially benefit from New York's taxicab monopoly, while highly organized, are relatively few in number. They are the taxi-medallion owners, those in allied trades, and politicians who receive campaign contributions. On the other hand, those who bear the burden of the monopoly are large in number: the taxicab riders of New York City, who receive lower-quality service and pay higher prices for it, plus would-be entrants into the taxi business.

The recognition that government-sponsored monopolies might be race-neutral also tells us that blacks who already own taxis are just as likely to support collusions as are whites. Everybody likes a monopoly in what they sell and competition in what they buy. Taxis aside, blacks who are part of a monopolized market structure, such as a licensed trade or occupation or a union-protected job, will share the same interest in maintaining a collusion as do whites.

Economically, the solution to some of the problems of upward mobility that many blacks face is relatively simple. The more difficult problem lies in the political arena: how to reduce or eliminate the power of interest groups to use government to exclude? The broad solution to exclusion is for the U.S. Supreme Court to interpret the right to work as it now interprets the right to speech. The Court has all but said that there is no compelling state reason for limiting freedom of speech. Similarly, from a moral point of view, there are very few compelling state reasons for limiting one's freedom to work.

One of the most eloquent statements of that position was stated by Supreme Court Justice Rufus W. Peckham, when he wrote the Court's unanimous opinion in *Allgeyer v. Louisiana* in 1897: "The liberty mentioned in that amendment [Fourteenth] means not only the right of the citizen to be free from the mere physical restraint of his person, as by incarceration, but the term is deemed to embrace the right of the citizen to be free in the enjoyment of all his faculties; to be free to use them in all lawful ways; to live and work where he will; to earn his livelihood by any lawful calling; to pursue any livelihood or avocation, and for that purpose to enter into all contracts which may be proper, necessary and essential to his carrying out to a successful conclusion the purposes above mentioned."[10]

Notes

Chapter 1 • Blacks Today and Yesterday

1. Department of Commerce, Census Bureau, "Poverty: Poverty Threshold 2006," *Current Population Survey, 2006 Annual Social and Economic Supplement,* table A1, www.census.gov/hhes/www/poverty/data/threshld/thresh06.html (accessed May 5, 2010).

2. Robert Rector, "Food Fight: How Hungry Are America's Children?" *Policy Review* (Fall 1991): 38–43.

3. Rector and Kirk Johnson, "Understanding Poverty and Economic Inequality in the United States," *Heritage Foundation Backgrounder #1713* (January 5, 2004), www.heritage.org/Research/Welfare/bg1796.cfm (accessed May 5, 2009).

4. Rector, "Poverty in U.S. Is Exaggerated by Census," *The Wall Street Journal,* September 25, 1990, A18.

5. www.cdc.gov/nchs/data/statab/t001x17.pdf. See also Thomas Sowell, *Ethnic America* (New York: Basic Books, 1981), 222; and June O'Neill, "The Changing Status of Black Americans," *The American Enterprise,* vol. 3, no. 5 (September/October 1992): 72.

6. Census Bureau, "Marital Status and Living Arrangements," *Current Population Survey* (Washington, D.C.: Government Printing Office, March 1998 Update), Series P-1, 20–514.

7. Census Bureau, *Current Population Reports,* Series P-20, no. 468 (Washington, D.C.: Government Printing Office, 1992), vi, cited in Thomas Sowell, *The Vision of the Anointed* (New York: Basic Books, 1995), 80.

8. Herbert Gutman, *The Black Family in Slavery and Freedom: 1750–1925* (New York: Pantheon Books, 1976), 10.

9. *The Black Family,* ix.

10. Ibid., xix.

11. Frank F. Furstenberg Jr., Theodore Hershberg, and John Modell, "The

Origins of the Female-Headed Black Family: The Impact of the Urban Experience,"
Journal of Interdisciplinary History VI:2 (1975): 211–233. Originally published in
Kenneth L. Kusmer, ed., *From Reconstruction to the Great Migration, 1877–1917*,
vol. 4, part II, (New York: Garland Publishing, 1991), 72–96.

12. "The Origins," 180.

13. Theodore Hershberg, "Free Blacks in Antebellum Philadelphia: A Study
of Ex-Slaves, Freeborn, and Socioeconomic Decline," *Journal of Social History* 5:2
(1971–72): 194.

14. Gutman, *The Black Family*, 449–56.

15. Sowell, *The Vision*, 81. Prior to 1890, this question was not included in the
census.

16. Rector, "Why Expanding Welfare Will Not Help the Poor," (lecture
no. 450, The Heritage Foundation, Washington, D.C., 1993), 6.

17. National Center for Health Statistics, *National Vital Statistics Report*, vol. 50,
no. 5 (Hyattsville, Md.: 2002), 49.

18. Charles Murray, "The Coming White Underclass," *The Wall Street Journal*,
October 29, 1993.

19. Gregory B. Christensen and Walter E. Williams, "Welfare Family Cohe-
siveness and Out of Wedlock Birth," *The American Family and the State*, ed. Joseph
Peden and Fred Glahe (San Francisco: Pacific Institute for Public Policy Research,
1986), 398.

20. M. Anne Hill and June O'Neill, "Underclass Behavior in the United States:
Measurement and Analysis of Determinants," cited in Rector, "Why Expanding
Welfare," 6.

21. Lawrence M. Mead, *The New Politics of Poverty: The Nonworking Poor in
America* (New York: Basic Books, 1992), 170.

Chapter 2 • Is Discrimination a Complete Barrier to Economic Mobility?

1. For an excellent discussion of immigrant groups see Oscar Handlin, *The
Uprooted* (New York: Grosset & Dunlap, 1951); J. C. Furnas, *The Americans* (New
York: G. P. Putnam's Sons, 1969); Nathan Glazer and Daniel Patrick Moynihan,
Beyond The Melting Pot (Cambridge, Mass.: MIT Press, 1963); and Thomas Sowell,
Ethnic America (New York: Basic Books, 1981), especially 51–92.

2. Bob Hepple, *Race, Jobs and the Law in Britain*, 2nd ed. (London: Penguin
Books, 1970), 20.

3. R. A. Schermerhorn, *Comparative Ethnic Relations* (New York: Random
House, 1970), 75.

4. Yosh Tandon, *Problems of a Displaced Minority: The New Position of East
Africa's Asians* (London: Minority Rights Group, 1972), 5.

5. The ironic aspect of this whole matter: anti-Asian feelings developed in spite

of Indian support and collaboration with the Africans in their struggles for independence. The Indians considered Mau Mau an orthodox struggle and sympathized with its aims; Indian newspapers voiced the opinions of black Africans and directly sponsored publication of their newspapers, assisted in African education, and were generally cooperative with the East Africans. But none of this overshadowed the rising intensity of African nationalism and African resentment of the Indian socioeconomic position in the territories. J. S. Mangat, *A History of the Asians in East Africa* (London: Oxford University Press, 1969): esp. 72–8.

6. Mangat, *A History of the Asians,* 15; In Uganda, in addition to the expulsion of the Asians, there has been a mass execution of the Langi and the Acholi by the Nubians. See John Humphreys, "Amin Promises Liberation, Delivers Exile and Murder," *Matchbox* (Spring/Summer 1975): 7–12.

7. Thomas Sowell, *Preferential Policies: An International Perspective* (New York: William Morrow & Co., 1990), 69–76.

8. Thomas Patrick Melady, *Burundi: The Tragic Years* (New York: Orbis Books, 1974), 34. See also Leo Kuper, *Genocide: Its Political Use in the Twentieth Century* (New Haven: Yale University Press, 1981), 63, 115, 164.

9. Memo dated November 15, 1994: Members of the independent inquiry into the actions of the United Nations during the 1994 genocide in Rwanda, addressed to the UN secretary-general, "Report of the Independent Inquiry into the action of the United Nations during the 1994 genocide in Rwanda," December 15, 1999.

10. In Burma, the Indians are even more despised. Moshe Yegar, *The Muslims of Burma: A Study of a Minority Group* (Wiesbaden, Germany: Otto Harrassowitz, 1972), 32.

11. Hugh Mabbett, *The Chinese in Indonesia, the Philippines and Malaysia* (London: Minority Rights Group, 1972), 19, 24.

12. Ibid., 5.

13. See T. H. Silcock, "The Effects of Industrialization on Race Relations in Malaya," in *Industrialization and Race Relations,* ed. Guy Hunter (New York: Oxford University Press, 1965), 177–200.

14. See Virginia Thompson and Richard Adloff, *Minority Problems in Southeast Asia* (Stanford, Calif.: Stanford University Press, 1955); and G. W. Skinner, *Leadership and Power in the Chinese Community of Thailand* (Ithaca, N.Y.: Cornell University Press, 1958).

15. Sowell, *Preferential Policies,* 46.

16. Mabbett, *The Chinese in Indonesia,* 25.

17. See Peter T. Bauer, *Reality and Rhetoric: Studies in the Economics of Development* (Cambridge, Mass: Harvard University Press, 1984), 7, 81.

18. Sowell, *Preferential Policies,* 50.

19. I might add that in the East African states of Kenya, Tanzania, and Uganda, before the expulsion of Asians, the Indians were an alien and politically powerless group. Yet they constituted an economically powerful middle class that owned large

industrial enterprises and controlled most of the retail activity. They have been discriminated against by both the Africans and the Europeans. See Yosh Tandon, *Problems of a Displaced Minority.*

20. Some observers of the Chinese problem in Southeast Asia assert that the resentment and hostility against the alien Chinese population stems from their success in the economic sphere. Contrast this assertion with that frequently made with regard to ethnic minorities in the United States—that they are *un*successful in the economic sphere because of white hostility and resentment.

21. Sowell, *Race and Economics* (New York: David McKay, 1975), 127.

22. See avalon.law.yale.edu/19th_century/chinese_exclusion_act.asp (accessed September 5, 2010).

23. Pauli Murray, *States' Law on Race and Color: Studies in the Legal History of the South* (Athens, Ga.: University of Georgia Press, 1997), 51.

24. William Petersen, "Chinese and Japanese Americans," in *Essays and Data on American Ethnic Groups,* ed. Thomas Sowell, (Washington, D.C.: The Urban Institute, 1978), 65–106.

    a. Toyosaburo Korematsu v. United States, *U.S. Supreme Court Reports,* 323 U.S. 214 (1944), no. 22, caselaw.lp.findlaw.com/scripts/getcase.pl?court=U.S.& vol=323&invol=214 (accessed November 15, 2002).

    b. Kiyoshi Hirabayashi v. United States, *U.S. Supreme Court Reports,* 320 U.S. 81 (1943), no. 870, www.tourolaw.edu/patch/Hirabayashi/Douglas.htm (accessed November 15, 2002).

    c. Ex Parte Mitsuye Endo v. United States, *U.S. Supreme Court Reports,* 323 U.S. 283 (1944), no. 70, www.bus.miami.edu/~jmonroe/endo.htm (accessed November 15, 2002).

25. D. E. Jaco and G. L. Wilber, Department of Labor, Bureau of Labor Statistics, "Asian Americans in the Labor Market," *Monthly Labor Review* (July 1975): 33–8.

26. Loren Schweninger, *Black Property Owners in the South 1790–1915* (Chicago: University of Illinois Press, 1990), 13.

27. Ibid.

28. Ibid.

29. Ibid., 8.

30. Ibid., 15.

31. Ibid., 16.

32. Ibid., 20–3.

33. E. Horace Fitchett, "The Traditions of the Free Negro in Charleston, South Carolina," *The Journal of Negro History,* vol. XXV, no. 2 (April 1940): 143; in *The Colonial and Early National Period,* ed. Kenneth L. Kusmer (New York: Garland Publishing, 1991), 299.

34. Eric Foner, *A Short History of Reconstruction* (New York: Harper & Row, 1990), 22.

35. Vishnu V. Oak, *The Negro's Adventure in General Business* (Westport, Conn.: Negro Universities Press, 1949), 41.

36. Robert C. Reinders, "The Free Negro in the New Orleans Economy, 1850–1860: Louisiana History," *The Journal of the Louisiana Historical Association*, vol. 6, no. 3: 278 and footnote 22.

37. "The Free Negro," 279.

38. Ibid., 274–5.

39. Ibid., 271.

40. Ibid., 276.

41. Schweninger, *Black Property Owners*, 39.

42. Ibid.

43. Ibid., 42.

44. Ibid., 44.

45. Ibid.

46. Ibid., 45.

47. Ibid., 11.

48. Ibid., 46.

49. Ibid., 48.

50. Ibid., 251.

51. Ibid., 50.

52. Ibid.

53. Ibid., 52.

54. Ibid., 53.

55. Laws of North Carolina, Chapter CXXVII, 102–3.

56. Schweninger, *Black Property Owners*, 53.

57. Roger A. Fischer, "Racial Segregation in Ante-Bellum New Orleans," *American Historical Review* 74:3 (1969): 928; in *Black Communities and Urban Development in America 1720–1990*, Kenneth L. Kusmer, ed. (New York: Garland Publishing, 1991), 83.

58. Marius Carriere Jr., "Blacks in Pre-Civil War Memphis," *Tennessee Historical Quarterly* 48:1 (1989): 6; cited in *Black Communities*, 124.

59. Schweninger, *Black Property Owners*, 55.

60. Ibid.

61. John Sibley Butler, *Entrepreneurship and Self-Help Among Black Americans* (New York: State University of New York Press, 1991), 38.

62. Oak, *The Negro's Adventure*, 39–40.

63. Butler, *Entrepreneurship and Self-Help*, 39.

64. Ibid.

65. Ibid., 40.

66. Ibid. See also Juliet E. K. Walker, "Racism, Slavery, and Free Enterprise: Black Entrepreneurship in the United States Before the Civil War," *Business History Review*, vol. 60 (Autumn 1986): 343–82.

67. Oak, *The Negro's Adventure,* 40.

68. Butler, *Entrepreneurship and Self-Help,* 42.

69. Oak, *The Negro's Adventure,* 39.

70. Pennsylvania *Register,* December 10, 1834, cited in Emma Jones Lapsansky, "'Since They Got Those Separate Churches': Afro-Americans and Racism in Jacksonian Philadelphia," *American Quarterly* 32:1 (1980): 61; in *Black Communities,* 315.

71. Leon F. Litwack, *North of Slavery: The Negro in the Free States, 1790–1860* (Chicago: University of Chicago Press, 1961), 159.

72. *North of Slavery,* 161.

73. Ibid., 163.

74. Ibid.

75. These advertisements are cited in Robert Ernst, "The Economic Status of New York City Negroes, 1850–1863," *Negro History Bulletin* 12 (1949): 133.

76. Ibid., 135.

77. Litwack, *North of Slavery,* 160.

78. Ibid., 172–73.

79. Ibid., 173.

80. Ibid., 175.

81. Butler, *Entrepreneurship and Self-Help,* 45. See also Schweninger, *Black Property Owners,* 47.

82. Ibid., 46.

83. Oak, *The Negro's Adventure,* 39–40.

84. Ibid.

85. Reinders, "The Free Negro," 285.

86. Isaac N. Carey v. The Corporation of Washington, V. Cranch (November, 1836); cited in Dorothy Provine, "The Economic Position of the Free Blacks in the District of Columbia, 1800–1860," *Journal of Negro History* 58:1 (1973): 66; Carey v. Washington, case no. 2,404, 5 Cranch, C.C. 13, Circuit Court D.C., November term, 1836, 5 Federal Cases, 62–66.

87. Harriet Johnson v. Corporation of Washington, 5 Cranch 13, November term, 1836; cited in Letitia Woods Brown, *Free Negroes in the District of Columbia 1790–1846* (New York: Oxford University Press, 1972), 135.

88. Provine, "The Economic Position," 67.

89. Ibid., 71.

Chapter 3 • Race and Wage Regulation

1. Department of Commerce, Bureau of the Census, *Negro Population, 1790–1950* (Washington, D.C.: Government Printing Office, 1918), 166, 503–4.

2. Richard K. Vedder and Lowell E. Galloway, *Out of Work: Unemployment*

and Government in Twentieth-Century America (New York: Holmes & Meir, 1993), 281.

3. Price V. Fishback, "Can Competition Among Employers Reduce Governmental Discrimination? Coal Companies and Segregated Schools in West Virginia in the Early 1900s," *Journal of Law and Economics* 32 (1989): 311–28.

4. Robert Higgs, *Competition and Coercion: Blacks in the American Economy, 1865–1914* (London: Cambridge University Press, 1977), 63.

5. *Competition and Coercion,* 64.

6. Ibid., 118.

7. Armand J. Thieblot, Jr., *Prevailing Wage Legislation: The Davis-Bacon Act, State "Little Davis-Bacon Acts," The Walsh-Healey Act, and the Service Contract Act.* (Philadelphia: The Wharton School, 1986), 140.

8. L. 1891 Ch. 114 p. 192–3.

9. House Committee on Labor, *Hearings on H.R. 7995 and H.R. 9232,* 71st Cong., 2d Sess. 17 (1930).

10. General Accounting Office, *The Davis-Bacon Act Should Be Repealed* (Washington, D.C.: Government Printing Office, 1979), 117.

11. Thieblot, *Prevailing Wage,* 28–9.

12. House Committee on Labor, *Hearings on Hours of Labor and Wages on Public Works,* 69th Cong., 2d Sess. 3 (1927).

13. Ibid.

14. *Hours of Labor.* Emphasis added.

15. Mark W. Kruman, "Quotas for Blacks: The Public Works Administration and the Black Construction Worker," *Labor History* 16 (Winter 1975): 38.

16. *Quotas for Blacks,* 38–9.

17. Ibid., 39.

18. Cong. Rec., 71st Cong., 3d Sess. 6,513 (March 31, 1931).

19. House of Representatives, *Hearings on H.R. 7995* (1931), 26–7.

20. Senate Committee on Manufacturers, *Hearings on S. 5904, Wages of Laborers and Mechanics on Public Buildings,* 71st Cong., 1931 (statement of AFL President William Green).

21. Cong. Rec., vol. 68, part 2 (January 18, 1927), 1,904.

22. Cong. Rec., House (February 28, 1931), 6,520.

23. Cong. Rec., House, 71st Cong., 3d sess. (1931), 6,513.

24. Ibid., 6,510.

25. Ibid., 6,516, 6,517, 6,520.

26. Robert Goldfarb and John Morrall, "The Davis-Bacon Act: An Appraisal of Recent Studies," *Industrial and Labor Relations Review* 34 (1981): 191–206; cited in Daniel S. Hammermesh and Albert Rees, *The Economics of Work and Pay* (New York: Harper & Row, 1984), 247.

27. James Sherk, "Davis-Bacon for Ethanol," www.heritage.org/Research/Labor/wm1562.CFM.

28. F. Ray Marshall, Allan M. Carter, and Allen G. King, *Labor Economics: Wages, Employment and Trade Unionism* (Homewood, Ill.: Richard D. Irwin, 1976), 240.

29. House Subcommittee on Labor Standards of the Committee on Education and Labor, testimony by the National Association of Minority Contractors (1986), 3.

30. Patrick Barry, "Congress's Deconstruction Theory," *The Washington Monthly,* January 1990, 2–3.

31. Vedder and Galloway, *Racial Dimensions of the Davis-Bacon Act* (Washington, D.C.: Heritage Foundation, 1990).

32. Vedder and Galloway, *Out of Work,* 279–80.

33. Scott Hodge, "Davis-Bacon: Racist Then, Racist Now," *The Wall Street Journal,* June 25, 1990, A14.

34. Barry, "Congress's Deconstruction," 11.

35. Steven Chapman, "Loss for Public Housing Tenants," *The Washington Times,* July 24, 1990, Commentary, 1.

36. Washington v. Davis (No. 74–1492), 168 U.S. App. D.C. 42, 12 F. 2d 956. reversed (1976).

37. Village of Arlington Heights v. Metropolitan Housing Development Corporation, 429 U.S. 252, 265, 97 S. Ct. 555, 563, 50 L. Ed. 2d 450 (1977).

38. Ibid.

39. Adkins v. Children's Hospital of District of Columbia, 261 U.S. 525 (1923).

40. West Coast Hotel Co. v. Parrish, 300 U.S. 379 (1937).

41. Americans victimized by antibusiness ideology largely misconceive the role and actions of businessmen. In the literal sense of the word, they are really employees. Their customers, acting collectively, are the employers. The fact that customers exhibit preferences for lower prices forces the businessman, if labor costs rise, to make adjustments that minimize production costs. If he does not make adjustments, he will lose his customers and/or investors to firms that do make them — because customers and stockholders are far from indifferent to prices and returns on equity, respectively.

42. The cost to the employer is actually higher because, in addition to wages, he pays fringe benefits such as Social Security and medical insurance, estimated to be roughly one-third of the money wage.

43. It is important to note that most people acquire marketable skills by working at a "subnormal wage," which amounts to paying to learn. For example, inexperienced doctors (interns), during their training, work for salaries that are a tiny fraction of what trained doctors earn. College students pass up considerable amounts of money in the form of tuition paid and income forgone in order to develop marketable skills. It is ironic, if not tragic, that low-skilled youths from

poor families are denied an opportunity to get a similar start in life. This is exactly what happens when a high minimum wage forbids low-skilled workers to "pay" for job training in the form of a lower beginning wage. It must be remembered that teenagers are not supporting families and in most cases are living at home, and hence could afford to pay for their training.

44. See, for example, J. Peterson and C. Stuart, *Employment Effects of Minimum Wages* (Washington, D.C.: American Enterprise Institute, 1969); J. Mincer, "Unemployment Effects of Minimum Wages," *Journal of Political Economy,* vol. 84, no. 4, part 2 (August 1976): 87; E. M. Gramlich, "Impact of Minimum Wages on Other Wages and Family Income," *Brookings Papers on Economic Activity,* no. 2 (1976): 409; F. Welch and J. Cunningham, "Effects of Minimum Wages on the Level and Age Composition of Youth Employment," *Review of Economics and Statistics,* vol. 60, no. 1 (February 1978): 140; J. P. Matilla, "The Impact of Minimum Wages on Teenage Schooling and on the Part-Time/Full-Time Employment of Youths," S. Rottenberg, ed. *The Economics of Legal Minimum Wages,* P. Linneman, *The Economic Impacts of Minimum Wage Laws: A New Look at an Old Question* (Chicago: University of Chicago Press, Center for the Study of the Economy and the State, 1980—mimeographed); J. F. Boschen and H. I. Grossman, "The Federal Minimum Wage, Employment, and Inflation," U.S. Minimum Wage Study Commission's *Report,* vol. VI (1981): 19; J. S. Pettengill, "The Long Run Impact of a Minimum Wage on Employment and on the Wage Structure," *Report,* vol. VI, 64; J. C. Cox and R. L. Oaxaca, "Effects of Minimum Wage Policy on Inflation and on Output, Prices, Employment, and Real Wages by Industry," *Report,* vol. VI, 195; C. Brown, C. Gilroy, and A. Kohen, "Effects of the Minimum Wage on Youth Employment and Unemployment," *Report,* vol. V, 2; J. Heckman and S. Sediacek, "The Impact of the Minimum Wage on the Employment and Earnings of Workers in South Carolina," *Report,* vol. V, 253; D. Hammermesh, "Employment Demand: The Minimum Wage and Labor Costs," *Report,* vol. V, 27; B. M. Fleisher, "Comments," *Report,* vol. V, 85; R. H. Meyer and D. A. Wise, "Discontinuous Distributions and Missing Persons: The Minimum Wage and Unemployed Youth," *Report,* vol. V, 198; J. R. Behrman, P. Taubman, and R. Sickles, "The Short and Long run Effects of Minimum Wages on the Distribution of Income," *Report,* vol. VII, 105–6; and W. R. Johnson and E. K. Browning, "Minimum Wages and the Distribution of Income," *Report,* vol. VII, 31–2.

Also L. P. Datcher and G. C. Lourh, "The Effect of Minimum Wage Legislation on the Distribution of Family Earnings Among Blacks and Whites," *Report,* vol. VII, 125–6, 149. See also: Douglas K. Adie, "Teenage Unemployment and Real Federal Minimum Wages," *Journal of Political Economy* 81 (1973): 435–41; David Neumark and William Wascher, *Evidence on Employment Effects of Minimum Wages and Subminimum Wage Provisions from Panel Data on State Minimum Wage Laws* (Cambridge, Massachusetts: National Bureau of Economic Research Working Paper no. 3859, 1992); Charles Brown, Curtis Gilroy, and Andrew Kohen, "The Effect of Minimum Wages on Employment and Unemployment," *Journal of Economic Literature* 20 (1982): 482–528; David E. Haun, "Minimum Wages, Factor Substitution, and the Marginal Producer," *Quarterly Journal of Economics* (August 1965): 478–86; Yale Brozen, "The Effect of Statutory Minimum Wages on Teenage Unemployment," *Journal of Law and Economics* (April 1969): 109–22; Marvin Kosters and Finis Welch, "The Effects of Minimum Wages on the Distribution of Changes in Aggregate Employment," *American Economic Review* (June 1972): 323–32; William G. Bowen and T. Aldrich Finegan, *The Economics of Labor Force Participation* (Princeton, N.J.: Princeton University Press, 1969); Edmund S. Phelps, *Inflationary Policy and Unemployment Theory* (New York: W. W. Norton and Co., 1972); Arthur F. Burns, *The Management of Prosperity* (New York: Columbia University Press, 1966); Thomas G. Moore, "The Effect of Minimum Wages on Teenage Unemployment Rates," *Journal of Political Economy* (July/August 1971): 897–902; James F. Ragan, Jr., "Minimum Wages and the Youth Labor Market," *The Review of Economics and Statistics* (May 1977): 129–36; Martin Feldstein, "The Economics of the New Unemployment," *The Public Interest* (Fall 1973); and Andrew Brimmer, *Minimum Wage Proposals, Labor Costs, and Employment Opportunities in the Nation's Capitol* (Washington, D.C.: Brimmer & Company, 1978), demonstrates the adverse employment and business migration effects of the minimum wage law in Washington.

45. J. R. Kearl, et al., "What Economists Think," *American Economic Review*, vol. 69, no. 2 (May 1979): 30.

46. Richard M. Alston, J. R. Kearl, and Michael B. Vaughn, "Is There Global Economic Consensus: Is There a Consensus Among Economists in the 1990's?" *American Economic Review*, vol. 82, no. 2 (May 1992): 204.

47. See, for example, G. L. Bach, *Economics*, 10th ed. (Englewood Cliffs, N. J.: Prentice Hall, 1980), 526; P. Samuelson, *Economics*, 11th ed. (New York: McGraw-Hill, 1980), 369–70; R. G. Lipsey, *An Introduction to Positive Economics* (London: Weidenfeld and Nicolson, 1963), 308–9; A. A. Alchian and W. R. Allen, *University Economics* (Belmont, Calif.: Wadsworth, 1964), 485–6; R. Attiyeh et al., *Basic Economics* (Englewood Cliffs, N. J.: Prentice-Hall, 1973), 87–8; F. Benham, *Economics: A General Introduction* (London: Sir Isaac Pitman & Sons, 1960), 318; R. T. Bye, *Principles of Economics*, 5th ed. (New York: Appleton Century-Crofts, 1956), 489; S. T. Call and W. L. Holahan, *Microeconomics* (Belmont, Calif.: Wadsworth, 1980), 420, 433; R. Campbell, *People and Markets, An Introduction to Economics* (Menlo Park, Calif.: Benjamin-Cummings, 1978), 268–71; R. Chisholm and M. McCarty, *Principles of Economics* (Glenview, Ill.: Scott, Foresman, 1978), 340; C. E. Ferguson and J. P. Gould, *Microeconomic Theory*, 4th ed. (Homewood, Ill.: Richard D. Irwin, 1975), 470–2; J. E. Hibdon, *Price and Welfare Theory* (New York: McGraw-Hill, 1969), 378–80; R. G. Lipsey and P. O. Steiner, *Economics*, 4th ed.

(New York: Harper and Row, 1975), 108–10; E. Mansfield, *Microeconomics, Theory and Applications,* 3rd ed. (New York, W. W. Norton, 1979), 383; W. Nicholson, *Intermediate Microeconomics and its Applications,* 2nd ed. (Hinsdale, Ill.: Dryden Press, 1979), 380–3.

48. General Accounting Office, "Minimum Wage Policy Questions Persist," *Report to the U.S. Senate Committee on Labor and Human Resources* (1983).

49. Congressional Budget Office, *Cost Estimate for H.R. 1834* (Washington, D.C.: Government Printing Office, March 25, 1988), 2.

50. Beryl W. Sprinkel, chairman, Council of Economic Advisors, letter to Representative Thomas E. Petri, May 13, 1988.

51. David Card and Alan B. Krueger, "Minimum Wages and Employment: A Case Study of the Fast-Food Industry in New Jersey and Pennsylvania," *American Economic Review,* vol. 84, no. 4 (September 1994): 772–93.

52. David Card and Alan B. Krueger, *Myth and Measurement: The New Economics of the Minimum Wage* (Princeton, N.J.: Princeton University Press, 1995).

53. See www.epionline.org/study_epi_njfast_04-1996.pdf.

54. David Neumark and William Wascher, *The Effect of New Jersey's Minimum Wage Increase on Fast-food Employment: A Re-evaluation using Payroll Records* (Cambridge, Mass.: National Bureau of Economic Research, 1995).

55. House-Senate Joint Economic Committee, "Raising the Minimum Wage: The Illusion of Compassion," *Economic Update,* April 1996, www.house.gov/jec/cost-gov/regs/minimum/illusion.htm.

56. Monroe H. Brown, ed., *The Fairmont Papers* (San Francisco: Institute for Contemporary Studies, 1981): 50.

57. Census data indicate a remarkable closing of the educational gap, measured in median years of education, between blacks and whites. In fact, the difference is negligible, with median years for blacks 12.2 and whites 12.5. However, possession of a high school diploma is not synonymous with the ability to read, write, and perform simple numerical calculations. The Coleman Report said that blacks at grade twelve lagged three to five years behind whites in terms of academic achievement.

58. G. V. Doxey, *The Industrial Colour Bar in South Africa* (London: Oxford University Press, 1961), 112.

59. Ibid., 156. Emphasis added.

60. "Rightest South Africans Assail Racial Job Curb," *The New York Times,* November 29, 1972, 3. In the United States, "liberals" are virtually unanimous in their condemnation of South African policy; yet they and black political leaders support some of the same labor policies and union practices that are supported in South Africa and used to handicap blacks. Interestingly, it is U.S. "conservatives" who reject, as applicable to the United States, South African labor and union policy.

61. Edward Roux, *Time Longer than Rope: A History of the Black Man's Struggle for Freedom in South Africa* (Madison, Wis.: The University of Wisconsin Press, 1964).

62. G. M. E. Leistner and W. J. Breytenbach, *The Black Worker of South Africa* (Pretoria: The African Institute, 1975), 28.

63. Ibid. Rate-for-the-job is the same as our equal-pay-for-equal-work laws.

64. Doxey, *The Industrial Colour Bar*, 155.

65. Merle Lipton, *Capitalism and Apartheid: South Africa, 1910–84* (Totowa, N.J.: Rowman & Allanheld, 1985), 189.

66. Armen A. Alchian and Reuben A. Kessel, "Competition, Monopoly, and the Pursuit of Pecuniary Gains," H. Gregg Lewis, ed., *Aspects of Labor Economics* (Princeton, N.J.: Princeton University Press, 1962).

67. The federal minimum wage is only one of the minimum wages that actually or in effect are imposed in the United States. For example, union collective bargaining agreements, the Davis-Bacon Act, and other statutes are tantamount to the imposition of a wage minimum.

68. The assumption here, certainly valid in the contemporary United States, is that the purchasers of the firm's final product do not care whether it was produced by white or black workers.

69. The assumption here is that people are legally free to enter the market and that there are many employers—of domestic workers, car washers and manufacturing operatives, for example—who would hire them.

70. The effectiveness of the wage demand also depends upon the elasticity of the substitution of capital for labor, i.e., the extent to which machines can be substituted for labor.

71. Union support for these programs may explain why minorities and their political leaders give unions strong political support. Such support gives the impression that unions are prominority. Thus, in an important sense, minorities are captured union constituents. If they do not politically support the union goals that put them out of work in the first place, unions will not support the government handouts that minorities receive as a result of being out of work.

72. John F. Kennedy, "New England and the South: The Struggle for Industry," *Atlantic Monthly*, January 1954, 33.

73. Cong. Rec., House, 11, 383 (1966).

74. Congressional Budget Office, "The Minimum Wage: Its Relationship to Incomes and Poverty," staff working paper, June 1986, 24.

75. Robert R. Nathan, *The Impact of Increasing the Minimum Wage on Employment in Retailing* (Washington, D.C.: Robert R. Nathan Associates, July 1987), 17.

76. Department of Labor, Bureau of Labor Statistics, *Current Population Survey: 1992 Annual Averages*, unpublished tabulations.

77. Economists recognize this premise as zero elasticity of demand for labor

when employers are completely unresponsive to changes in wages. When this is true, employers will hire the same number of workers without regard to the wages they are paid.

Chapter 4 • Occupational and Business Licensing

1. There is little distinction to be made between the licensing of occupations and that of businesses. Licensing a taxi regulates the behavior of the driver; licensing a café, that of the owner.

2. Morris M. Kleiner, "Occupational Licensing," *Journal of Economic Perspectives* (Fall 2000): 190.

3. Simon Rottenberg, ed., *Occupational Licensure and Regulation* (Washington, D.C.: American Enterprise Institute for Public Policy Research, 1980), 2.

4. Bernard Siegan, *Economic Liberties and the Constitution* (Chicago: University of Chicago Press, 1980), 202.

5. Department of Labor, *Occupational Licensing and the Supply of Nonprofessional Labor*, Manpower Monograph no. 11 (Washington, D.C.: U.S. Department of Labor, 1969).

6. Siegan, *Economic Liberties*, 202.

7. Lee Behman, "Demand for Occupational Licensure," *Occupational Licensure*, Simon Rottenberg, ed., (1980) 13–25.

8. For a more complete discussion of these and other effects of licensing, see Rottenberg, "Economics of Occupational Licensing," in *Aspects of Labor Economics, a Report of the National Bureau of Economic Research* (Princeton, N.J.: Princeton University Press, 1962), 3–20.

9. Rottenberg, *Occupational Licensure*, 8.

10. New York City Administrative Code (Supp. 1969), para. 436-2.0.

11. Gilbert Gorman and Robert E. Samuels, *The Taxicab: An Urban Transportation Survivor* (Chapel Hill, N.C.: University of North Carolina Press, 1982), 92; www.ci.nyc.ny.us; www.nypost.com/seven/05302007/news/regionalnews/600g_medallion_not_too_shabby_cabby_regionalnews_paul_tharp.htm (accessed September 17, 2010).

12. See www.nyc.gov/html/tlc/html/misc/avg_med_price.shtml (accessed September 17, 2010)

13. Interview with loan officer of a New York City bank, who requested anonymity.

14. See www.medallionfinancial.com/news-release-5-29-07.htm (accessed September 17, 2010)

15. Technically, the license price can be approximated by:

$$\sum_{i=1}^{n} \frac{R_i^r - R_i^o}{(1+r)^i},$$

where the superscripts *r* and *o* are receipts in a restricted and open market respectively. Thus, $R^r - R^o$ is the difference in receipt accruing from a protected market. The denominator is the interest rate that yields the present value.

16. William Mellor, "Is New York City Killing Entrepreneurship?" www.ij.org/about/component/content/2248?task=view (accessed September 17, 2010).

17. For the entire United States from 1980 to 2002, see www.taxi-liberty.org/safety.htm (accessed September 25, 2010).

18. "Illegal Livery Street Hail Study," prepared for Taxi Policy Institute, January 2002. www.schallerconsult.com/taxi/.

19. Charles Vidich, *The New York Cab Driver and His Fare* (Cambridge, Mass.: Schenkman Publishing, 1976), 148.

20. Ibid., 146.

21. Debra Lam, et al., "The San Francisco Taxicab Industry: An Equity Analysis, 2006," www.taxi-library.org/goldman2006.pdf (accessed September 18, 2010).

22. Leroy Jones, Ani Ebong, Rowland Nwankwo, Girma Molalegne, Quick Pick Cabs, Inc., and Reverend Oscar S. Tillman v. Robert Temmer, Christine Alvarez, and Vincent Majkowski, acting in their official capacities as members of the Colorado Public Utility Commission. Plaintiffs' Response to Defendants' Motion to Dismiss, or in the Alternative, for Summary Judgment. Civil Action no. 93-235 in U.S. Dist. Ct. (Dist. of Colo.), 12.

23. Leroy Jones, et al., attached affidavits of the plaintiffs.

24. In the writer's opinion, this practice differs little from such criminally extortionary practices as protection-money payments to old-time mob bosses.

25. See www.dctaxi.dc.gov/dctaxi/lib/dctaxi/pdf/dcmr/31_D.C.MR_chapter_10.pdf (accessed September 18, 2010)

26. See House Subcommittee on Public Utilities, Insurance and Banking, Committee on the District of Columbia, *Taxicab Industry in the District of Columbia,* 85th Cong. (1957), 425.

27. House Committee on the District of Columbia, staff report on taxicab regulation (Washington, D.C., 1976), 281.

28. Ibid., 278–296.

29. Fingleton, et. al., *The Dublin Market: Reregulate or Stay Queueing?* (Dublin: Economics Department, Trinity College, 1997), 6. Cited in Sean D. Barrett, "Regulatory Capture, Property Rights and Taxi Deregulation: A Case Study," *Journal of The Institute of Economic Affairs,* vol. 23, no. 4 (Oxford, England: Blackwell Publishing, 2003), 34.

30. "Regulatory Capture," 35.

31. Ibid., 38.

32. See ij.org/component/content/article/35-economicliberty/817-ny-vans-background (accessed September 18, 2010). See also Darrin Schlegel, "Jitney drivers ready to roll again on city streets," *Houston Business Journal,* May 9, 1994.

33. Institute for Justice, *Liberty & Law*, vol. 8, no. 2 (May 1999): 1. See also Institute for Justice website, www.ij.org.

34. Transcript of the City Council of New York, June 30, 1993, 39–41.

35. Transcript of the City Council of New York, November 22, 1993, 28.

36. Transcript, June 30, 1993, 117.

37. Transcript of the City Council of New York, December 21, 1993, 201–2.

38. Stuart Dorsey, "The Occupational Licensing Queue," *Journal of Human Resources*, vol. 15 (Summer 1980).

39. Matthew Shofield, "Great Wichita Hair Debate," *The Kansas City Star*, July 4, 1993.

40. In states such as Texas, California, Ohio, and South Carolina, investigators, often accompanied by police, have raided hair-braiding shops, arresting proprietors and intimidating patrons. See Lisa Jones, "Hair Police State," *The Village Voice* (New York, September 22, 1998).

41. Sidney L. Carroll and Robert J. Gaston, "Occupational Restrictions and the Quality of Service Received," *Southern Economic Journal* 47 (1981): 959–76.

42. Alex Maurizi, "Occupational Licensing and the Public Interest," *Journal of Political Economy* (March 1974): 399–413.

43. See Thomas G. Moore, "The Purpose of Licensing," *Journal of Law and Economics* (October 1961): 93–117.

44. Walter Gellhorn, "The Abuse of Occupational Licensing," *Chicago Law Review*, vol. 6, no. 2, 44.

45. "The Abuse," 11–12.

Chapter 5 • Excluding Blacks from Trades

1. Lorenzo Greene and Carter G. Woodson, *The Negro Wage Earner*, (Washington, D.C.: The Association for the Study of Negro Life and History, 1930), 192.

2. Sterling D. Spero and Abraham L. Harris, *The Black Worker: The Negro and the Labor Movement* (New York: Kennikat Press, 1931), 477–8.

3. *The Black Worker*, 478–9.

4. Cited in *The Black Worker*, 480.

5. Cited in *The Black Worker*, 481.

6. Greene and Woodson, *The Negro Wage Earner*, 320.

7. Ibid.

8. Spero and Harris, *The Black Worker*, 68.

9. Thomas O'Hanlon, *Fortune*, January 1968, 172.

10. Isaac Weld, *Travels Through the States of North America and the Providences of Upper and Lower Canada*, vol. I (London: J. Stockdale, 1799), 145–52.

11. James Weldon Johnson, *Along This Way* (New York: Viking, 1937), 32.

12. Cited in Herbert Hill, "The Racial Practices of Organized Labor," Arthur

M. Ross and Herbert Hill, eds., *Employment, Race and Poverty* (New York: Harcourt Brace & World, 1967), 375.

13. John Stephen Durham, "The Labor Unions and the Negro," *Atlantic Monthly,* February 1898, 226.

14. Ibid.

15. Ibid., 227.

16. Hill, "The Racial Practices," 378.

17. Ibid., 379.

18. Herbert R. Northrup, *Organized Labor and the Negro* (New York: Harper & Bros., 1944), 1–5.

19. Charles S. Johnson, "Negro Workers and the Unions," *The Survey,* April 15, 1928, 114. Cited in David E. Bernstein, "Roots of the 'Underclass': The Decline of Laissez Faire Jurisprudence and the Rise of Racist Labor Legislation," *The American University Law Review,* vol. 43, no. 1 (Fall 1993): 113.

20. W. E. B. Dubois, "The Denial of Economic Justice to Negroes," *The New Leader,* February 9, 1929, 43, 46. See also Dubois, "The Economic Future of the Negro," *Publications of the American Economic Association,* 3rd series, vol. 7, no. 1 (February 1906): 219–242,

21. Spero and Harris, *The Black Worker,* 135.

22. Kelly Miller, "The Negro as a Workingman," *American Mercury,* November 1925, 310, 313.

23. Bruce Grit, *The Colored America* (October 18, 1902), cited in Bernstein, "Roots of the 'Underclass,'" 92.

24. Frederick Douglass, "The Tyranny, Folly, and Wickedness of Labor Unions, *New National Era* (March 23, 1871), cited in Robert L. Factor, *The Black Response to America* (Reading, Mass.: Addison-Wesley, 1970), 45; Booker T. Washington, "The Negro and the Labor Unions," *Atlantic Monthly,* June 1913, 753–56.

25. William Julius Wilson, *The Declining Significance of Race* (Chicago: University of Chicago Press, 1980), 150; Edna Bonacich, "A Theory of Ethnic Antagonism: The Split Labor Market," *America Sociology Review,* vol. 37 (1972), 547, 553, cited in Bernstein, "Roots of the 'Underclass'": 93.

26. Johnson, "Negro Workers," 113–14.

27. John P. Roche, *The Quest for the Dream: The Development of Civil Rights and Human Relations in Modern America* (New York: Macmillan, 1963), 22.

28. Bernstein, "Roots of the 'Underclass,'" 114.

29. John G. Van Duesen, "The Black Man in White America," *The Journal of Negro History,* vol. 24, no. 1 (January 1939): 123–25.

30. This section relies heavily on material drawn from William M. Tuttle, Jr., "Labor Conflict and Racial Violence: The Black Worker in Chicago, 1894–1919," *Labor History* 10:3, (1969): 408–32, reprinted in *From Reconstruction to the Great Migration, 1877–1917,* vol. 4, pt II, ed. Kenneth L. Kusmer (New York: Garland Publishing, 1991), 72–96.

31. "Labor Conflict," 76.

32. Ibid.

33. Ibid., 77.

34. Ibid., 85.

35. Ibid., 91.

36. Ibid.

37. National Industrial Recovery Act, Pub. L. 48, ch. 10, 195.

38. Harvard Sitkoff, *A New Deal for Blacks: The Emergence of Civil Rights as a National Issue* (New York: Oxford University Press, 1978), 58, 330–35.

39. Raymond Wolters, *Negroes and the Great Depression: The Problem of Economic Recovery* (Westport, Conn.: Greenwood Press, 1970), 122–23.

40. Raymond Wolters, "Section 7a and the Black Worker," *Labor History,* vol. 10 (1969): 459, 466.

41. Sitkoff, *A New Deal for Blacks,* 55.

42. Herbert Hill, *Black Labor and the America Legal System* vol. I, in *Race, Work, and the Law* (Washington, D.C.: The Bureau of National Affairs, 1977), 100.

43. A. L. A. Schechter Poultry Corporation v. United States, 295 U.S. 495 (1935).

44. Melvin I. Urofsky, *The March of Liberty: A Constitutional History of the United States* (New York: Alfred A. Knopf, 1988), 671.

45. Hill, *Black Labor,* 100.

46. Raymond Wolters, "Closed Shop and White Shop: The Negro Response to Collective Bargaining 1933–1935," *Black Labor In America,* ed. Milton Cantor (1969), 137, 149.

47. Philip Foner, *History of the Labor Movement in the United States: The Policies and Practices of the America Federation of Labor, 1900–1909* (New York: International Publishers, 1964), 215.

48. Sitkoff, *A New Deal for Blacks,* 52.

49. Morgan O. Reynolds, *Power and Privilege* (New York: Universe Books, 1984), 125.

50. NLRB v. Jones & Laughlin Steel Corporation, 301 U.S. 1, 30.

51. Larus & Brother Company, 62 NLRB 1075, 1083 (1945).

52. Atlanta Oak Flooring Company, 62 NLRB 973, 975 (1945).

53. Richard K. Vedder and Lowell E. Gallaway, *Out of Work: Unemployment and Government in Twentieth-Century America* (New York: Holmes & Meier, 1993), table 1.3, 8.

54. Gunnar Myrdal, *An American Dilemma* (1944), 397–98.

55. Benjamin Shimberg, et al., *Occupational Licensing* (Washington, D.C.: Public Affairs Press, 1973), 112–13.

56. *Occupational Licensing,* 113.

57. Ibid., 123.

58. Equal Employment Opportunity Commission, news release, May 19, 1970.

59. Commission on Civil Rights, *The Challenge Ahead: Equal Opportunity in Referral Unions* (Washington, D.C.: Government Printing Office, May 1976), 25.

60. Herbert Hammerman, "Minority Workers in Construction Referral Unions," *Monthly Labor Review* (May 1972): 17–26.

61. Alex Maurizi, "Occupational Licensing and the Public Interest," *Journal of Political Economy* (March 1974): 399–413.

62. Spero and Harris, *The Black Worker*, 269.

63. Ray Marshall, *The Negro Worker* (New York: Random House, 1967), 57.

64. Department of Commerce, *Census of the Population: 1940*, vol. 3, *The Labor Force*, pt. I, table 62.

65. Cited by Herbert Hill, "The Racial Practices of Organized Labor," in *Employment, Race*, 203.

66. Letter from C. E. Pane, "Negro vs. White Firemen," *Locomotive Firemen's Magazine*, August 1899, 203–4.

67. Despite a general consensus among today's public that people should be paid identically if they do identical work, this law is the first step toward handicapping the most disadvantaged group of workers. Pushing for equal wages was the same strategy employed by racist labor unions in South Africa's mining industry. See Walter E. Williams, *South Africa's War Against Capitalism* (New York: Praeger Books, 1989), 71–3.

68. Spero and Harris, *The Black Worker*, 291.

69. Ibid., 293. Emphasis added.

70. Hill, "The Racial Practices," 15; Spero and Harris, *The Black Worker*, 291.

71. Spero and Harris, *The Black Worker*, 291.

72. Ibid., 296–8.

73. Hill, "The Racial Practices," 15. See also John M. Matthews, "The Georgia Race Strike of 1909," *Journal of Southern History*, vol. 40 (1974): 613, 617–21.

74. 158 U.S. 564, 599, 600 (1895).

75. Erdman Act of June 1, 1898, 30 Statute 424, ch. 370, para. 10, 428 (1898).

76. 208 U.S. 161, 173, 180.

77. 236 U.S. 1, 26 (1915).

78. Senate Committee on the Judiciary, hearings on "Limiting Scope of Injunction in Labor Disputes," 70th Cong., 1st Sess. (1927), 609–14.

79. Railway Labor Act of 1926, Title 45 — United States Code, ch. 347, 44 Statute 577; and amended as Railway Labor Act of 1934, ch. 691, 48 Statute 1185.

80. Railway Labor, 1,185 and 1,187.

81. Spero and Harris, *The Black Worker*, 22; Ray Marshall, "The Negro in Southern Unions," *The Negro and the American Labor Movement*, ed. Julius Jacobson (New York: Doubleday and Company, 1968), 128, 134–35.

82. 137 F2d 817 (D.C. Cir. 1943), rev., 320 U.S. 715 (1943).

83. Brotherhood of Railway and Steamship Clerks v. UTSEA, 137, F. 2nd 817, 78 (U.S. Ct App. D.C. 125, August 2, 1943).

84. For additional problems and examples, see Howard W. Risher, Jr., *The Negro in the Railroad Industry* (Philadelphia.: University of Pennsylvania Press, 1971), especially chapters 4–7.

85. Steele v. Louisville & NR Co., 323 U.S. 192, 202–203 (1944).

86. 245 Ala. 113,16 So. 2d 416, reversed.

87. Steele, 145.

88. Risher, *The Negro in the Railroad Industry*. 159–64.

89. Tunstall v. Brotherhood of Locomotive Firemen and Enginemen, 323 U.S. 210 (1944).

90. Charles H. Houston, "Foul Employment Practices on the Rails," *Crisis* (October 1949): 269–84.

91. Samuel Gompers, "Talks on Labor," *American Federalationist* 12 (September 1905): 636, 638.

92. Hill, "The Racial Practices," 389.

93. Ibid., 390.

94. Ibid.

95. *Samuel Gompers' Paper: The Making of a Union Leader,* ed. Stewart B. Kaufman, vol. 1 (Chicago: University of Illinois Press, 1986), 300–1.

96. *Samuel Gompers' Papers,* 390–1.

97. William B. Gould, *Black Workers in White Unions* (Ithaca, N.Y.: Cornell University Press, 1977).

98. See Franks v. Bowman Transportation Co., 495 F 2d 398 (5th Cir.), cert. denied, 419 U.S. 1050(1974); U.S. v. Navaho Freight Lines, Inc., 525 F 2d 1318 (9th Cir. 1975); Hairston v. McLean Trucking Co., 520 F 2d 226 (4th Cir. 1975); U.S. v. T.I.M.E. - D.C., Inc., 517 F 2d 299 (5th Cir. 1975); Saba v. Western Gillette, Inc., 516 F 2D 1251 (5th Cir. 1975); Rodriguez v. East Texas Motor Freight, Inc., 505 F 2d 66 (5th Cir. 1974); Herrara v. Yellow Freight Systems, Inc., 505 F 2d 66 (5th Cir. 1974); U.S. v. Lee Way Motor Freight, Inc., 505 F 2d 69 (5th Cir. 1975); Bing v. Roadway Express, Inc., 444 F 2d 687 (5th Cir. 1971); U.S. v. Lee Motor Freight, Inc., 6 FEP Cases 274 (C.D. Cal. 1973).

99. Gould, *Black Workers in White Unions,* 369.

100. United States v. Pilot Freight Carriers, Inc., 6 FEP Cases 280 (M.D., N.C., July 30, 1973) and United States v. Navajo Freight Lines, Inc., 6 FEP Cases 274. (C.D. Cal. June 6, 1973).

101. United States v. Lee Way Motor Freight, Inc., 6 FEP Cases 274 (C.D. Cal., 1973).

102. "Bias in the Cab," *The Wall Street Journal,* March 31, 1966, 1 and 6.

103. FEP Cases at 745 and 7 FEP Cases at 729.

104. With employers of truck drivers, many Teamsters locals had formal or

informal exclusive-hiring arrangements that required employers to hire drivers on a referral basis from the union hall. That gave wide scope for racial discrimination.

105. John S. Heywood and James H. Peoples, "Deregulation and the Prevalence of Black Truck Drivers," *Journal of Law and Economics,* vol. XXXVII (April 1994): 139

106. "Deregulation and the Prevalence," 141, 148.

107. Ibid., 141.

108. Ibid., 149.

109. Ibid., 150.

110. Ibid., 134.

111. Interstate Commerce Commission, *Report on Minority Participation in the Surface Transportation Industry Ex Parte,* no. MC-150 (Sub-No. 1) (Washington, D.C.: Interstate Commerce Commission, July 1981), 1.

112. James D. Gwartney, Richard Stroup, and A. H. Studenmund, *Microeconomics: Private and Public Choice* (New York: Harcourt Brace Jovanovich College, 1992), 290–91.

113. For additional summaries of deregulation results, see Thomas Gale Moore, "Transportation Policy," *Regulation* (1988), www.cato.org/pubs/regulation/regv12n3/reg12n3-moore.html (accessed September 20, 2010); Dennis W. Carlton and Jeffrey M. Perloff, *Modern Industrial Organization* (Glenview, Ill.: Scott, Foresman/Little Brown, 1990), 825–34; Daniel Machalaba, "More Companies Push Freight Haulers to Get Better Rate, Service," *The Wall Street Journal,* December 18, 1985, 1.

114. *Inc.* Magazine. CEO Fights Regulators, but Not Regulations. May 1980.

Chapter 6 • Racial Terminology and Confusion

1. Erica Frankenberg, Chungmei Lee, and Gary Orfield, *A Multiracial Society with Segregated Schools: Are We Losing the Dream?* (Cambridge, Mass.: The Civil Rights Project, Harvard University, 2003), 67.

2. According to a survey conducted by the Joint Center for Political and Economic Studies, a black, liberal-to-moderate, Washington-based think tank, 88 percent of blacks favor education "choice" plans that include public and private schools. The highest support, 95 percent, comes from blacks with incomes of less than $15,000. Overwhelming backing for various forms of educational choice among blacks, which includes tuition tax credits and vouchers, is found in polls compiled by the Department of Education's Center for Choice in Education for their report "Public Opinion on Choice in Education." The percentages of black support are: Georgia (57), Louisiana (64), Illinois (65), Wisconsin (83), Indiana (50), Detroit (53). A Lou Harris Poll published in *Business Week* (September 14, 1992) reported that 63 percent of Americans think that "Children should be able to attend any

school they qualify for including public, parochial, or private schools, with government money going to poor or middle-income children attending" either of the latter two. A Gallup Poll found that 51 percent of the public in general support educational vouchers, while among blacks the figure is 72 percent.

3. Department of Commerce, Bureau of the Census, *Subject Reports* on marital status for 1960, 1970, and 1980; and *Current Population Report* P20, nos. 461 and 468, table 1, www.census.gov/population/socdemo/race/interractab1.txt (accessed September 26, 2010).

4. See www.webpresidentsusa.com/AP060303.htm (accessed September 25, 2010).

5. Assortive or nonrandom selection of mating partners with respect to one or more characteristics is positive when like people mate more frequently than would be expected by chance and is negative when the reverse occurs.

6. Gary S. Becker, "A Theory of Marriage: Part I," *The Journal of Political Economy*, vol. 81, no. 4. (July–Aug. 1973): 813–46. Mating of "likes"—positive assortive mating—is extremely common, whether measured by intelligence, height, skin color, age, education, family background, or religion, although unlikes sometimes also mate, as measured, say, by an inclination to nurture or succor, to dominate or be deferential. This suggests that traits are typically but by no means always complementary (See Becker, 827.)

7. Kenneth J. Arrow, "What Has Economics to Say About Racial Discrimination?" *Journal of Economic Perspectives*, vol. 12, no. 2 (Spring 1998): 91.

8. Khiara M. Bridges, "Note on the Commodification of the Black Female Body: The Critical Implications of the Alienability of Fetal Tissue," *Columbia Law Review* 102 (January 2002): 143.

9. Adarand Constructors, Inc. v. Pena (1995) 115 S.Ct. 2097, 243. Emphasis added.

10. Diabetes Foundation of Mississippi, Inc., "A High Risk Group—Native Americans Prevalence," www.msidabetes.org/nativeamericans/html (accessed July 24, 2003).

11. University of Maryland Medicine, "Urological Disorders: Prostate Cancer" (May, 2003), 2g.isg.syssrc.com/urolology-info/proscan.html (accessed July 24, 2003).

12. "Latest News: The Expanding Racial Scoring Gap Between Black and White SAT Test Takers," *The Journal of Blacks in Higher Education* (2002), www.jbhe.com/latest/37_b&w_sat.html (accessed July 24, 2003).

13. Jon Entine, *Taboo: Why Black Athletes Dominate Sports and Why We Are Afraid to Talk about It* (New York: Public Affairs, 2000), 31.

14. Department of Justice, Bureau of Justice Statistics, "Homicide Trends in the U.S. Trends by Race" (2002), www.ojp.gov/bjs/homicide/race.htm#ovrelrace (accessed July 24, 2003).

15. Washington Lawyers Committee for Civil Rights and Urban Affairs, "Public Accommodations: Taxicab Discrimination," *Washington Lawyers Committee Update,* vol. 9, no. 1 (Spring 2003), www.washlaw.org/news/update/public accommodations spring 2003.htm_ (accessed July 24, 2003).

16. James Owens, "Capital Cabbies Salute Race Profiling" (1999), home.net com.com/~owensva/cabbie.html (accessed July 24, 2003).

17. Stephen Rosamond, "What Do You Say or Do in a Public Relations Nightmare," *PMQ Pizza Marketing Quarterly,* www.pmq.com/pr_nightmare.shtml (accessed July 24, 2003).

18. Jeffrey Goldberg, "The Color of Suspicion," *The New York Times,* June 20, 1999, www.jeffreygoldberg.net/articles/nyt/the_color_of_suspicion.php (accessed July 24, 2003).

19. Ibid.

20. Federal Bureau of Investigation, *Crime in the United States, 2006: Uniform Crime Reports,* www.fbi.gov/ucr/cius2006/data/table_43.html (accessed July 24, 2003).

21. This is not completely true: one report estimates that approximately 2,600 Negroes become white—i.e., "pass"—each year. See E. W. Eckard, "How Many Negroes Pass?" *American Journal of Sociology,* vol 52, no. 6 (May 1947): 498–500.

22. Abigail Thernstrom, "The Racial Gap in Academic Achievement," *Beyond the Color Line: New Perspectives on Race and Ethnicity in America* (Stanford, Calif.: Hoover Press, 2002).

23. *National Center for Education Statistics, 2009, Digest of Education Statistics,* nces.ed.gov/programs/digest/d09/tables/dt09_143.asp.

24. Michael Fix and Margery Turner, "Testing for Discrimination: The Case for A National Report Card," *Civil Rights Journal* (Fall 1999), www.questia.com/googleScholar.qst?docId=5001896870 (accessed September 25, 2010).

25. The cost of providing auto insurance to women is 50 percent that of men, resulting in women traditionally being charged a premium 60 percent of that charged men. Providing insurance to a 45-year-old woman is 16 percent lower than for a man of the same age. See Daniel Seligman, "Insurance and the Price of Sex," *Fortune,* February 21, 1983, 84–5.

26. Glenn B. Canner and Delores S. Smith, "Home Mortgage Disclosure Act: Expanded Data on Residential Lending," *Federal Reserve Bulletin,* vol. 77 (November 1991): 859–61. See also, Alicia Munnell, et al., *Mortgage Lending in Boston: Interpreting the HMDA Data,* working paper (Boston: Federal Reserve Bank of Boston, 1992): 92–97. Since mortgage-denial rates for whites are 6 percent less than for blacks, this study claims that the difference is due to racial discrimination.

27. Paulette Thomas, "Federal Data Detail Pervasive Racial Gap in Mortgage Lending," *The Wall Street Journal,* March 31, 1992, 1, A10.

28. Julianne Malveaux, "The Future of Urban Areas," *The Black Scholar,* vol. 23, no. 1 (Winter/Spring 1993): 12.

29. Jesse Jackson, "Racism is the Bottom Line in Home Loans," *Los Angeles Times,* October 28, 1991, B5.

30. Department of Commerce, Bureau of the Census, *Household Wealth and Asset Ownership: 1984,* Current Population Reports, Household Economic Studies, series P-70, no. 7 (July 1986), 4–5. See also, William Bradford, "Wealth, Assets and Income in Black Households," working paper, vol. 1, no. 1 (Afro-American Studies Program, University of Maryland, 1990).

31. Bureau of the Census, Economics and Statistics Administration, *Net Worth and Asset Ownership of Households: 1998 and 2000,* 2.

32. *Net Worth,* 14.

33. Canner and Smith, "Expanded HMDA Data on Residential Lending: One Year Later," *Federal Reserve Bulletin,* vol. 77 (November 1992): 808.

34. Peter Brimelow and Leslie Spencer, "The Hidden Clue," *Forbes,* January 4, 1993, 48.

35. www.freddiemac.com/corporate/reports/cceipoll.htm.

36. Raphael Bostic, "A Test of Cultural Affinity in Home Mortgage Lending" working paper (U.S.C. Lusk Center for Real Estate, February 2002), 37.

37. Walter E. Williams, "Some Hard Questions on Minority Businesses," *Negro Educational* Review, vol. XXV, nos. 2 and 3 (April/July 1974): 123–42; Andrew F. Brimmer, "The Black Banks: An Assessment of Performance and Prospect," *The Journal of Finance,* vol. 26, no. 2 (May 1971): 379–405.

38. Edward M. Gramlich, "Subprime Mortgage Lending: Benefits, Costs, and Challenges," speech delivered at the Financial Services Roundtable Annual Housing Policy Meeting, Chicago, Illinois, May 21, 2004, www.federalreserve.gov/boarddocs/Speeches/2004/20040521/default.htm#table, table 3 (accessed September 26, 2010).

39. See www.federalreserve.gov/boarddocs/Speeches/2004/20040521/default.htm#table, table 3 (accessed September 26, 2010).

40. Carrie Teegardin, "Black Atlantans Often Snared By Subprime Loans," *Atlanta Journal-Constitution,* November 4, 2007, forums.allsexresources.com/showthread.php?t=138315 (accessed September 26, 2010).

41. Editorial, "Subprime in Black and White," *The New York Times,* October 17, 2007, www.nytimes.com/2007/10/17/opinion/17wed2.html (accessed September 26, 2010).

42. See David Caplovitz, *The Poor Pay More* (New York: Free Press of Glencoe, 1967); Warren G. Magnuson and Jean Carter, *The Dark Side of the Market Place* (Englewood Cliffs, N.J.: Prentice-Hall, 1968); Frederick Sturdivant, "Better Deal for Ghetto Shoppers," *Harvard Business Review,* vol. 46 (March–April 1968):

130–9; Frederick Sturdivant and Walter Wilhelm, "Poverty, Minorities and Consumer Exploitation," *Social Science Quarterly*, vol. 49 (December 1968): 643–50.

43. Federal Trade Commission, *Economic Report on Installment Credit and Retail Sales Practices of District of Columbia Retailers* (Washington, D.C.: Government Printing Office, 1968).

Chapter 7 • Summary and Conclusion

1. Cited in Robert Higgs, *Competition and Coercion: Blacks in the American Economy 1865–1914* (London: Cambridge University Press, 1977), 48.

2. Ibid.

3. Ibid.

4. Ibid.

5. Jay J. Coakley, *Sports in Society* (New York: Times-Mirror Magazine, 1986), 145.

6. *The NBA's Official Encyclopedia of Pro Basketball*, ed. Zander Hollander (New York: New American Library, 1981), 151.

7. Barry D. McPherson, "The Black Athlete: An Overview and Analysis," *Social Problems in Athletics: Essays in the Sociology of Sports*, ed. Daniel M. Landers (Urbana, Ill.: University of Illinois Press, 1976), 131.

8. Armen Alchian and William R. Allen, *Exchange and Production: Competition, Coordination and Control*, 2nd ed. (Belmont, Calif.: Wadsworth Publishing, 1977), 322.

9. For a more thorough examination of these principles, see Harold Demsetz, "Minorities in the Market Place," North Carolina Law Review, vol. 43 (February 1965): 271–99; Alchian and Reuben Kessel, "Competition, Monopoly, and the Pursuit of Pecuniary Gain," *Aspects of Labor Economics* (Princeton, N.J.: Princeton University Press, 1962).

10. Allgeyer v. State of Louisiana, 165 U.S. 589 (1897).

About the Author

BORN IN PHILADELPHIA, PENNSYLVANIA, Walter E. Williams holds a BA in economics from California State University, Los Angeles, and MA and PhD degrees in economics from the University of California at Los Angeles. Williams has served on the faculty of George Mason University in Fairfax, Virginia, as the John M. Olin Distinguished Professor of Economics, since 1980; from 1995 to 2001, he served as department chairman. He has also served on the faculties of Los Angeles City College, California State University, Los Angeles, and Temple University in Philadelphia, and Grove City College, Grove City, Pennsylvania.

Williams is the author of numerous publications that include books as well as articles that have appeared in scholarly journals, such as *Economic Inquiry, American Economic Review, Georgia Law Review, Journal of Labor Economics, Social Science Quarterly,* and *Cornell Journal of Law and Public Policy,* and popular publications, such as *Newsweek, Ideas on Liberty, National Review, Reader's Digest, Cato Journal,* and *Policy Review.*

Williams has received many fellowships and awards including Foundation for Economic Education's Adam Smith Award, Hoover Institution National Fellow, Ford Foundation Fellow, Valley Forge Freedoms Foundation's George Washington Medal of Honor, Veterans of Foreign Wars U.S. News Media Award, Adam Smith Award, California State University's Distinguished Alumnus Award, George Mason University Faculty Member of the Year, and Alpha Kappa Psi Award.

Index